A How To Guide to Cosmopolitan Socialism

A Tribute to Michael Brooks

A How To Guide to Cosmopolitan Socialism

A Tribute to Michael Brooks

Matthew McManus

Winchester, UK
Washington, USA

JOHN HUNT PUBLISHING

First published by Zero Books, 2023
Zero Books is an imprint of John Hunt Publishing Ltd., No. 3 East St., Alresford,
Hampshire SO24 9EE, UK
office@jhpbooks.com
www.johnhuntpublishing.com
www.zero-books.net

For distributor details and how to order please visit the 'Ordering' section on our website.

ISBN: 978 1 78279 316 8
978 1 78279 317 5 (ebook)
Library of Congress Control Number: 2021944049

A CIP catalogue record for this book is available from the British Library.

Design: Stuart Davies

UK: Printed and bound by CPI Group (UK) Ltd, Croydon, CR0 4YY
Printed in North America by CPI GPS partners

We operate a distinctive and ethical publishing philosophy in
all areas of our business, from our global network of authors to
production and worldwide distribution.

Contents

Also by the Author
What is Post-Modern Conservatism, Zero Books,
ISBN 978-1-78904-245-0

Dedicated to Michael Jamal Brooks. Solidarity Brother

Acknowledgments

This book was written in the midst of the COVID 19 epidemic, which exposed how fragile the neoliberal order of governance truly is. We realized that the people holding society together are those so readily ignored by power – nurses, grocery store clerks, bus drivers, caregivers and so on. We all owe them a tremendous debt of gratitude. More specifically I would like to thank my wife, Marion Trejo, and my family for all the help they've given, especially Adam McManus and Kayla Patrick who provided a home while we weathered the storm. Thanks to Whitman College and Tec de Monterrey for keeping me gainfully employed. Thank you to Donna Brooks for chatting with me about Michael Brooks' legacy, and providing me with some of the resources needed to flesh out his conception of cosmopolitan socialism. And most especially thanks to Michael Brooks, a fellow Zero Book author and commentator who passed away shortly before this was written. Michael was that rare beast – a genuinely cool guy and deep soul who also produced bang up online content. We on the left are much the poorer for his loss and have a duty to carry on his legacy.

Introduction by Ben Burgis

Michael Brooks died in the summer of 2020.

The author of the book you're holding now, Matt McManus, is a good writer and a sharp thinker and I fully expect *Cosmopolitan Socialism* to reach a significant and appreciative readership. But the potential audience for a book like this would have been ten times larger if Michael had lived until 2030 or even 2025 instead of 2020.

The day he died, I got a text message from Bhaskar Sunkara—a friend of both Michael's and mine and our editor at *Jacobin*. He asked me how I was taking the news. When I told him I didn't know what he was talking about, he called me. The rest of the world found out a few hours later.

In the following days tributes were posted on Twitter and YouTube by everyone from Glenn Greenwald (already, in the summer of 2020, a *bette noire* of American liberals) to conventionally left-liberal MBNC commentator Chris Hayes to more than a few self-described "communists." Most strikingly, one came in from former Brazilian president Lula da Silva—a figure who loomed sufficiently large in the relatively short time I was close to Michael that we'll have to come back to him in a minute.

The write-ups I saw in mainstream media outlets were at most a few paragraphs long. They always got his age wrong. (Everyone was subtracting 1983 from 2020. This was July, though, and his thirty-seventh birthday would have been in August.) That his death was noted at all on, for example, CNN's website says something about the state of his career when he died. So does the fact that writers at these outlets seemed so unsure about what to say.

For a substantial window into the man you had to read *Jacobin*, which ran a seemingly endless series of tributes from friends and comrades in Michael's democratic socialist extended political family. In Bhaskar's contribution, he talked about how he would meet Michael for drinks and get to hear some of the impressions and characters beloved to the audience of Michael's YouTube show and podcast TMBS (The Michael Brooks Show) as well as some private ones just for him—like a bit Michael developed, in what Bhaskar described as a very good Indian accent, where he imitated Bhaskar's parents being disappointed that their son was wasting his time running a communist magazine instead of trying to make some money.

Given the range of Michael's interests and the intensity with which he connected with people he met at different stages of his short life, those who met him at different times sometimes seem to remember very different Michaels. Friends who knew him for far longer than I did had often bonded with him over his deep interest in silent meditation and "spirituality"—interests that I respect but do not even begin to share. By the time he crossed my path, that facet of who he was and what he did remained interesting and intriguing but it wasn't front and center in quite the same way.

The first conversation I ever had with Michael Brooks was in line at a Chipotle in Boise, Idaho. We were both attending a conference organized by Doug Lain, who was then the editor of Zero Books, in collaboration with a local group in Idaho. Michael and I both had book contracts with Zero. Mine was for *Give Them An Argument: Logic for the Left*, and I'd already finished a draft. Michael's was for *Against the Web: A Cosmopolitan Answer to the New Right*, and at that point what he had was mostly a chaotic and often genuinely brilliant hodge-podge of ideas.

We hadn't exactly met yet but we both ended up in a group of conference participants going out to grab lunch. Standing in line, Michael and I somehow got to talking about Donald Trump and ended up admitting to each other that, as much as we both reviled him as a president, we both enjoyed him as an insult

2

comic. Once we got outside, everyone sat around a plastic table eating burritos and talking about Jordan Peterson—the subject of the conference and eventually one of the primary subjects of Michael's book. Anyone who watched Michael's show knows how much he enjoyed "dunking" on the Petersons of the world. What I sometimes think many people missed, though, is how serious he could be about *understanding* them.

His project in *Against the Web* was not just to mock these jackasses, although he certainly did some of that there, but to pierce through the outer layers of bullshit to reveal something not just about them but about reactionary thought in general— and hence about the struggle for social progress. A major theme of the book is that reactionaries like Peterson and his "Intellectual Dark Web" co-thinkers like Sam Harris and Ben Shapiro habitually try to either "naturalize" or "mythologize" unjust social hierarchies, using "science" or mysticism or both to try to treat contingent human institutions as somehow being part of the fabric of the universe. Think about Peterson's habit of babbling about eternally masculine Order and the eternally feminine Dragon of Chaos when railing against everyone from Marxists whose pursuit of "equality of outcome" allegedly threatens the freedom and prosperity of the West to blue-haired college kids who want Peterson to remember their preferred pronouns. Or think about Harris's use of crude utilitarian morality to defend everything from profiling Muslims at the airport to the possible "necessity" of the West steeling itself to use nuclear weapons in the Middle East—and his truly bizarre insistence that he's derived this moral system not from reflecting on his values but from objective "science."

An hour or two later Doug showed up and took both of us out for afternoon drinks and we talked more, political and theoretical and serious over beers in the darkness of the bar and convivial and crass and joke-y during the walk through the afternoon sunlight back to the conference. Michael and I pretty much kept talking until he flew back to Brookyln a couple days later.

That weekend there was a strange tempest-in-a-teapot controversy about a video Doug had made for the Zero Books YouTube channel presenting a Marxist critique of the limits of intersectional theory. A couple of other conference participants interpreted the point of the video uncharitably, and a lot of my conversation with Michael that weekend was us bonding over that—mostly Michael perfecting a comedy bit skewering the critics as only he could and me howling with laughter. But that was interspersed with intense discussions of everything from psychology to spirituality to Marxist theory to the concept of objective truth to the limits of social democratic reformism, the feel of it all like a vastly better version of an all-night session talking about ideas in a college dorm room. I was coming out of years in which I'd largely put my political interests on the backburner, and I was starting to take a real interest for the first time in my life in going out into the world to do debates and lectures and immerse myself in public-facing political commentary. Michael had already been doing all of that for years and years, but he was excited about his forthcoming book and seizing the opportunity to immerse himself in a weekend of more theoretical discussions. There was a side of Michael that could have easily become a history professor instead of a professional political pundit, and he was reveling in the chance to focus on that side of himself at this conference.

We both, I think, enjoyed the combination of shared politics and shared theoretical interests and a shared sense of no-holes-barred inappropriate humor. While he was much funnier than I'll ever be, I had my moments—and he seemed to like seeing exactly how much I would crack up over his most wildly "problematic" lines. He was, back then, a much harsher critic than I was of the self-defeating pathologies of our comrades on the Left, telling me for example that if the American Left ever had to go up to the mountains like Castro's guerillas, we'd never be able to do it because of all the arguments that would break out about whether going up to the mountains was "ableist."

At the time, my wife and I lived in central New Jersey, where we both taught classes at Rutgers University. When I was in the airport, getting ready to fly home, Michael sent me an audio clip he'd recorded of himself doing the comedy bit he'd perfected all weekend—basically, a version of Doug's video that would have been bad enough to justify the criticism. He sent it to me because he knew it would make me laugh but I'm sure that another part of the point was that it was a gesture of trust. The accompanying note playfully told me not to "play in front of woke people."

To be clear, Michael was deadly serious in his support for gay and trans rights, for cultural pluralism, and for the rights of religious and racial minorities. As Wosny "Big Wos" Lambre once put it to me in a reflective conversation, our late mutual friend was about as "into" the black struggle as any white boy he'd ever known. Michael had thoughtful things to say about the history of the civil rights movement, about the way the Southern Christian Leadership Conference types with their ties and their starched shirts and their social democratic policy agendas had a more enduringly radical legacy than the fire-breathingly revolutionary "Black Power" types who rose up in opposition to them, and he was borderline obsessed with the history of the struggle against apartheid. His frequently expressed distaste for the humorlessness, bad analysis, and alienating excesses of contemporary American "wokeness" had many sources—but one thing it can't be traced to is indifference to oppression or the kind of "class reductionism" the socialist left is sometimes accused of by liberals. In fact everything I've tried to express in this paragraph is the kind of thing that Michael had a way of making you understand in passing, as a matter of course, without needing to spell it out.

In the coming months, I'd often take the train into Brooklyn to meet Michael for dinner or drinks. These were the months that I'd started doing weekly videos for the Zero Books YouTube channel—sometimes commenting on news events but often just breaking down some terrible right-wing argument then in circulation. Many of them were about the same reactionary figures who preoccupied Michael.

He and I hadn't started working together yet. That would slowly develop in the subsequent months. In these early days, though, we rarely talked about *The Sopranos* or personal or professional developments the way we would so much later—it was pretty much all politics and theory (and jokes about politics and theory) all the time. I'd orient myself toward whatever was going on in the world that week by leaning on his political intuition and he'd work through his more abstract ideas.

Michael's personal, political, and professional influence on me would be difficult to overstate, and by the time he died I'd come to think of him as one of my closest friends—but I also realize that my understanding of him as a person is based on a very small slice of his life. What I *can* say is that the Michael Brooks I knew is the one who was just starting to come into his own as a political commentator, and that I had a front row seat while he was thinking through the ideas about "cosmopolitan socialism" that Matt works out a scholarly version of (or homage to) in this book.

As 2018 turned into 2019, we started to work together on many different fronts. I started doing a weekly segment called "the Debunk" on TMBS. Typically, I'd take on some terrible conservative or libertarian argument and explain in detail why it failed. "Taxation is theft?" Nope. Terrible circular argument— it assumes that rich people have a moral right to the wealth they currently possess in the first place. Can education and upward mobility fix poverty? Nope. Education only confers an advantage in the labor market because of its scarcity—and if everyone did somehow magically get a white-collar job no one would grow the food or drive it to grocery stores and we'd all starve to death.

Later on, when the Democratic primaries started, the targets were often anti-Bernie arguments made by centrist candidates and their supporters. Did Kamala or Mayor Pete say something asinine about Medicare for All last night? Were Tulsi Gabbard's supporters more interested in watching her workout videos with their jaws open than thinking about the asinine things she said at the last debate? We'd skewer it in the Debunk segment. More often than not, I was cast as the earnest philosophical straight man to Michael's standup comedy act, making my way through the arguments while he riffed, but when Michael laughed at one of your jokes it was the most validating reaction you could ever hope for—because when he thought something was funny his whole body would convulse with laughter. Some of the moments from those segments that linger the most brightly in my memory—full color, full sound—are the points when I'd say something a little bit funny in my dry nerdy way while Michael might be in the act of taking a drink and the beer bottle would pause on its way to his mouth and you could see him start to light up and I knew I'd gotten him. It's a small thing but almost two years after the last of the Debunks I can't think about that without wanting to cry.

Eventually, we also co-wrote several articles for *Jacobin* and I started to play a role as a first reader and informal editor for some of his other writing. Most importantly, though, a few months after we met he asked me to read the pages that had already been produced for his book *Against the Web*—and what started out as a feedback eventually became a much more direct role in the writing process.

I've never had any trouble thinking of it as "his" rather than "our" book. He exercised as much creative control as a director does on a set. I'm someone who shot some footage for his movie but, stretching the metaphor a little, not only did Michael decide on the final cut but we always had very long conversations about what he wanted for every shot. I can remember a point in the summer of 2019 when I'd regularly spend all day and all night in his apartment in Brooklyn working on some of those chapters. Sometimes he'd dictate passages. I'd rework the prose a bit, read them back to him, and he'd want changes and we'd repeat the process again and again. When we were done with it, pages would often go to our friend and comrade Daniel Bessner (who was also, I should say, something of an assistant director on *Against the Web*) for more revising and sometimes substantial rewriting and then come back to us. Michael was an instinctively collaborative person, always looking for ways that he could harness the talent and energy of a variety of people who, he thought, had something valuable to contribute.

Other times I'd initially write some pages, I'd read *those* out loud, he'd make insertions and we'd go from there. The whole thing could easily last from breakfast to the middle of the night while Michael's long-term girlfriend (who I won't name since she's a very private person) puttered around the apartment, cooking or studying or just hanging out, and occasionally got in on the discussion. It would be hard to remember later, during the pandemic when he often seemed subdued and depressed, but at the time the level of energy he displayed for this and the rest of his projects felt inhuman. I don't believe he had any inkling of how little time he had left—he could he?—but sometimes he acted as though he did.

As exhausting as this writing process could be, even at the time I found it thrilling—and, even more so now that he's gone, the chance to work that closely with him helping him get down on paper the ideas that mattered most to him feels like a gift. You probably have a sense of what I mean if you never met the man but you "just" watched or listened to him on TMBS and his other shows (he was the host or co-host of four of them by

Introduction by Ben Burgis

the end) or read the articles he co-wrote for *Jacobin* with me or his other regular co-authors, Djene Bajalan and Danny Bessner. If Michael's voice on a podcast feed or his image on YouTube *wasn't* a regular presence in your life during those years, it can be hard to convey quite what either socially or parasocially hanging out with him and hearing his perspective on ideas and events could feel like.

He was funny and charismatic, obviously—even more so off-air, if only because he was so boisterously unfiltered when he didn't have to worry about the more easily offended part of his audience misinterpreting him. But there was more to it than that. Much more. As you heard him talk, he had a way of making you *feel* the way he was sizing up different ideas, different ideological perspectives, different tactical "takes" on day-to-day politics and weighing them against each other so that when he finally arrived at a judgment—and that's the way to put it, a "judgment"—you intuitively *got* why he was landing where he did.

He was a passionate admirer, for example, of the Cuban Revolution. One time when I was preparing to talk about Cuba's impressive response to COVID-19 on a TMBS segment, he even told me to skip all the usual democratic socialist caveats about the undesirable features of Cuba's political system—not because he disagreed but because he wanted to keep the spotlight on the heroism of Cuba's response. This is a country, after all, that's been under a 60-year embargo by its largest natural trading partner—a trading partner that also happens to be the exclusive manufacturer of many important medical supplies—and still manages to send doctors all over the world to help suffering people. Another time, though, in a postgame discussion with me and Bhaskar and the TMBS crew, he casually mocked American leftists who pretend that—with all their boisterous and cranky opinions—they wouldn't have a problem with submitting to the equivalent of Cuba's censorship regime. In both cases, it was

9

impossible not to immediately and viscerally see the point.

Somehow the funniest person I knew and the person who was the most casually contemptuous of taboos of all kinds was also in a very real way the most serious and deeply thoughtful person that I knew. He had a way of pulling you in so you found yourself caring about the things he cared about—like an airborne infection of political and ideological passion.

I started listening to TMBS shortly before I met the man. My grad school friend Mark Warren recommended the show to me, telling me that Michael seemed to share a lot of my concerns about how to make the Left more strategic and appealing. He was right. And of course the recurrent bits like "Right-Wing Mandela" and "Nation of Islam Obama" cracked me up and the show had all the same parasocial attractions to me it had for the rest of his audience. But it had already been on air for almost a year and I tend to be a completist about shows I really like and so I started from the beginning.

By the third or fourth time I heard Michael talk about former Brazilian president Lula da Silva, though, I was a little sick of it. It's not that I disagreed with his perspective about the chain of events that led to Lula's imprisonment—the "lawfare coup" in which the Brazilian Right removed Lula's successor as leader of the Workers Party, Dilma Rousseff, from the presidency, the dubious investigation and railroading of Lula himself, the roots of it all in the Brazilian elite's loathing for what was by any reasonable standards a pretty moderately reformist administration, and the US connection to it all. It's that, out of everything that could be covered in a globe seething with injustice, I felt no special connection to this particular story. I wondered how often he was going to return to it. Somewhere along the way, though, without quite realizing it, I got invested in the story to the point that, after I met Bhaskar on the TMBS set one of the days I was doing the show in person—usually I did the Debunk via Skype or Zoom—the first article I wrote for

Jacobin ended up being about Brazil.

Part of why Michael responded in the way he did to the figure of Lula had to do with his deep identification with liberation movements in the global south and with movements for dignity and equality everywhere. A detail that's always stuck in my head about the deep hatred for Lula on the Brazilian Right despite the relatively mild nature of his social democratic reforms, is that wealthy Brazilians would often complain that— as a result of the Workers Party's efforts to essentially create a middle class in the country—"the airports are starting to look like bus stations." At the end of a live show we did at the Bell House in Brooklyn shortly before the pandemic started, he showed a clip of Lula speaking to a crowd shortly before he had to report to prison, orating in a way that sounded oddly dreamy despite having a voice as gravely as Tom Waits, and quoting Che Guevara talking about how the powers that be can kill a few flowers but they can't stop the coming of spring. That kind of thing spoke to Michael in a deep way.

But he also liked the way that Lula cut through political nonsense and ideological obfuscation and communicated in the kind of direct, visceral way so few American leftists seem to be any good at—the way he'd talk about making sure poor Brazilians had money to buy coffee and free time to watch soccer. Michael was, as much as anything else, a strategist, always thinking about how to make radical ideas mainstream.

For that purpose, he thought it was important to find what (with heavy irony, given his hatred for Clintonism and Blairism) he called a "third way" in the culture wars, a vision of how people could interact and live together free of bigotry but also free of petty moralistic micro-policing of individual behavior. He had nothing but contempt, for example, for the idea that "cultural appropriation" was a thing. All culture should equally be at the disposal of all humans.

I can remember, far more vividly than I can remember many

significant events in the two years since Michael died, sitting in a restaurant he liked in Brooklyn hearing him intensely discourse about this point to make sure I got what he was going for in *Against the Web*. And I can remember sitting outside a cottage in rural northern Michigan months later, drinking a Bell's Oberon and looking out at the dark woods, while we first talked about *The Sopranos* — a favorite non-political non-philosophical topic — and then he went back to the same theme.

Michael was an instinctive synthesizer of ideas. He had a knack not just for seeing the flaws and limitations of a perspective—that's the easy part!—but for cutting through to whatever core component of a flawed perspective still manages to be correct and compelling, and to put that core together with similar components harvested elsewhere. Matt's task in the book isn't made any easier by the fact that Michael's gift was far more for making conceptual connections vivid and compelling in *conversation*, both on- and off-air, than for spelling out the fine print.

I don't say that to denigrate his ability. I was in awe of how good he was at it, and two years after the last conversation any of us got to have with him I continue to find his insights compelling. But there's hard and necessary translation work to be done in order to make the ideas he was evoking explicit and examine them in detail. Matt's book is an excellent start. I can hope it'll be taken up by other writers, scholars, and commentators who see something valuable there and, through that process, some thread of the ideas Michael cared about can be kept alive.

Coda

It took me a very long time to compose the words you just finished reading. I wrote two articles about Michael within weeks of his passing, both of which can still be found at *Jacobin*. There was an attempt to distill some of his ideas called "The

Cosmopolitan Socialism of Michael Brooks" and before that an intensely personal reflection called "What Michael Brooks Meant to Me."

It was easy to write about him that summer. Somehow it even felt urgent—like I had to get it all down before I forgot a single precious detail. Now it took me months of delays to start a draft of this introduction, and I hated it, and it took me months to start again. A *year* has passed since Matt first asked me to take this on.

What it gets down to, I suppose, is this: Enough time has passed that I've really internalized that my favorite and closest collaborator, this human being I deeply loved, is never coming back. Writing about him now, every sentence feels like an acknowledgment of that awful truth, and it's like emptying an ashtray into my mouth and swallowing.

But it feels good to have said whatever I can get myself to say about him right now, and I want to just end by emphasizing this: Michael Brooks cared about the ideas you're about to read about because he cared about people. Whatever else you remember about him, remember that.

Preface

The first truly vivid political memory I have was 9/11. At the time I was in Grade Seven, living in Canada and mostly concerned about the kinds of things teenage boys tend to be concerned about. We were sent home, where my family and I watched the World Trade Center collapse on a nearly hypnotic rotation. My father had an intensely disturbed look in his eyes. Even though we were nowhere near New York or Washington, the whole city closed down. In the next few weeks the whole world seemed to change. A US president who had lost the popular vote and wasn't considered a paragon of self-determination began a series of wars that would destroy hundreds of thousands of lives and disrupt countless more for decades to come. Just a few short years later the largest economic collapse since the Great Depression took place, throwing millions out of their homes while some of the wealthiest people in the world received billions in unconditional bailouts. Not to be outdone, as I write this there is a pandemic sweeping the world that is sure to bring about tremendous suffering. We face a potential climate crisis which, far from being confronted head on, has been allowed to fester. All this is to say, contra the optimism of Stephen Pinker, that the globe in 2020 can appear a pretty messed up place.

None of this was supposed to happen. The conventional wisdom at the turn of 1989 was that history had come to an end, and all that was left to deal with was tinker around the edges of the neoliberal capitalist consensus. Interestingly it was American conservatives who initially pushed back hardest against this prospect; they of course wanted a world governed by capital, but not one that was devoid of opportunities for aggrandizement and the spectacular exercise of power. Consequently, the conservative reaction to the end of history – and consequently historical opportunities to exercise freedom

– and the advent of neoliberalism was to provide an ideological supplement in the form of neoconservatism. As Corey Robin observed in his classic *The Reactionary Mind*, neoconservatives welcomed the fall of the Soviet Union as an opportunity for the unbridled exercise of American power. But they also feared that unadulterated neoliberal materialism and cosmopolitanism would bring about a moral decline in the martial spirits of the American and other Western peoples. This anxiety was by no means unfounded given the ambition of neoliberals like Hayek was to overcome struggle and demands for the politics characteristic of historical time through the subordination of the demos to domestic and international law. This was partly out of residual Cold War animosity and partly out of a real commitment to the hierarchies and power relations established in competitive neoliberal societies, which were often glamorized with appeals to Straussian elitism. War outside was to a necessary excess in order to stabilize a potentially decadent liberal order within. The neoliberal rights to property and entrepreneurial subjectivity – tied to an insistence that you enjoy even the feeling of wanting something – had to be linked to a classical sense of martial responsibilities. The language of the 2000 Project for a New American Century Report on rearmament is telling. The neoconservative authors brush aside the claim that Americans should just "relax and live the good life" without confronting – or creating – new crises to face.

In other words, peace and prosperity were the harbingers of decline and fall. To preserve the existing order it was necessary to project an antagonistic and chaos inducing Other who would maintain the appearance of history restarting while paradoxically stabilizing capitalist realism at home. In this respect neoconservatism is consonant with the paradigm of liberal imperialist adventurism, which includes a long genealogy of Conradian harlequins from Disraeli through Kipling and Bush. At its peak neoconservatism prefaced the emergence of post-modern conservatism, with its insistence on conserving neoliberalism as home through transforming reality abroad. The post-modern simulacrum of history was to be maintained as a kind of hyperreal sport conducted by militarists in the developing world. Karl Rove's infamous dismissal of the "reality-based community" and his insistence that "we're an empire now, and when we act, we create our own reality" is telling. Since then the empire-building projects have collapsed due to repeated failures. But the post-modern conservative world order that the political right has turned to in its place is no better. Rather than externalizing the contradictions of neoliberalism abroad through neoconservative empire building, post-modern conservatives want to tear down the internationalist order to free themselves to reconstruct ethno nationalist polities from within. The enemies of the right, and the battles they seek, are not internal rather than externalized.

Through all this the left has struggled to provide an alternative vision of the international order that would be sufficiently compelling to compete and overcome those put forward by the political right. The consequence has been tremendous increases in inequality, economic chaos, needless wars and, increasingly, a rise in xenophobic myopia. The situation can't be allowed to continue. *Cosmopolitan Socialism: A How to Guide* is intended as a quick primer on how the left can begin to think globally, even if we must continue to act locally. It is inspired by Michael Brooks' vision of a better world, which sadly he never got to elaborate on since he passed away far too young in 2020. It is obviously not intended as definitive, since a globally minded left must obviously be sensitive to the extensive differences in history, culture and interests that mark the human species. But the book does insist that we need a left-wing approach to global politics and political economy that goes beyond just reacting to various right-wing agendas that are as ambitious as they are corrosive.

The book has four chapters. The first one discusses the

history of cosmopolitanism and its various critics. It then moves on to describing the history of left-wing internationalism in the early socialist and workers movements, and their occasionally friendly, occasionally hostile association with liberal internationalists focused on human rights and cosmopolitan institutions which emerged in the aftermath of the Second World War. The second chapter is on the collapse of left-wing and liberal internationalism, and the ascendency of neoliberalism as a global system of economic governance. This culminates with the collapse of the Soviet Union and the idea of the "end of history" where the neoliberal order was the sole global hegemon and destined to maintain that status forever. Chapter Three discusses the emergence of neoconservatism and later post-modern conservatism as right-wing reactions to the contradictions of global capitalism.

Chapter Four will be by far the longest and present my own arguments, following Michael Brooks, for what a cosmopolitan socialism would look like. It presents my arguments for why the political left was unable to successfully counter these right-wing efforts, partially because the ascendency of militant particularism as the guiding orientation of progressive activism precluded theorizing on how a globally minded left should operate. What came to matter were local and regional struggles – many of which were extremely valuable – but which were unable to coalesce into a genuine movement capable of challenging the status quo. One of our jobs will be to combine the localism of militant particularism with the internationalism of classical socialism. It would willingly draw inspiration from a variety of cultural sources, recognizing that the universality of struggles against reactionary hegemony may take many political forms. Cosmopolitan socialism would also seek to re-empower and democratize many of the international institutions developed in partnership with liberal internationalists while moving them in a progressive direction. The United Nations, the European Union and the international legal system all have the potential to be aligned with left-wing ambitions, so long as they become associated with the interests of world citizens rather than capital and the forces of reaction. A cosmopolitan socialism would also seek to overturn the efforts of neoliberal globalism to make the world safe for capital by insulating it from democratic and political pressure; particularly through a complex array of trade laws and powerful institutions which have removed themselves from the demos. We need to build civil society groups across borders which agitate for reform and the depoliticization of political economy at the national level. The political right has long held an advantage on this front, with post-modern conservative groups like The Movement and Baile Tusnad establishing a shared intellectual and political outlook to push against egalitarianism and reform. The political left needs to be as savvy to be globally effective. After this is accomplished, cosmopolitan socialism needs to entrench its accomplishments through international law and institutions, to ensure they both carry over generations and become established expectations If these steps were carried out we'd go a long way to creating a more just world that is, as Brooks would put it, kind to people but hard on systems of oppression.

This really is a global, collaborative endeavor...There is a shared working condition that's universal, and there are overlapping trajectories and aspirations and we can learn from each other.
Michael Brooks

Chapter One

Socialism, Liberalism and Cosmopolitanism

A Citizen of the World

I am human, and I think nothing human is alien to me.
Terence, Former slave and African-Roman playwright

Cosmopolitanism is far older than any of the great modernist doctrines: liberalism, socialism and conservative reaction. The roots of the word (surprise surprise) are in Ancient Greece. *Kosmos* referred variably or simultaneously to the "world" the "universe" or the celestial "cosmos." It is still the philological basis for cosmology; the branch of astronomy that deals with big issue questions like the origin of the universe and large-scale universal properties and physical laws. *Polites* means citizen, and is related to the word *polis*, which referred both to the physical center of a city and the urban community as a whole (the Greeks were less sticklers for the singular meaning of words than we were). Put together *kosmos* and *polites* becomes cosmopolitan: citizen of the world or cosmos. The bright guy who originated the term is usually taken to be the Greek philosopher Diogenes, who belonged to the cynical school of thought. Unlike today where a cynic is usually just a polite term for antagonistic asshole, in its classical usage it referred to a philosophy stressing the need to virtuously live in harmony with nature. When Diogenes claimed to be a "citizen of the world" he was expressing the view that the divide of humanity into separate and often warring polities was in a sense unnatural and unvirtuous. Many of these divisions were driven by what St Augustine would later call the libido dominandi: or the way the peoples and princes of one city lusted for domination over others. When Alexander the Great pridefully stood over the philosopher Diogenes, asking what gift a great king of men could offer a deep thinker, the cynic responded that the young aristocrat could stop blocking his sun. From the beginning cosmopolitanism looked sharply on the arbitrary accumulation of power in the hands of some over others and strove to wean us off the conceit that this was simply the way things must be.

The next major stream of cosmopolitan thinkers were the Stoics, who were not a little inspired by the transnational sweep of the Roman Republic (later the Roman Empire). They stressed that each human being existed in two communities at once: one the local community of her birth, and the next the community of all humankind. The Stoics also followed in Diogenes' footsteps in regarding the endless pursuit of power after power to be a mark of human pride and vanity. It all too often led to needless suffering and death, not to mention the corruption of the soul. Stoics like Seneca were also among the first to stress the fundamental equality of all human beings, beating both liberals and socialists by many millennia. This fed into their cosmopolitanism since they recognized that there was a fundamental arbitrariness to being born in this community or that community. This didn't make it morally unimportant, and most of the Stoics contended that our most immediate duties were to those closest to us. But it did weigh against treating well those near and like us as trumping all our duties to all those who shared our humanity. Not to be outdone, the Buddhist emperor Ashoka the Great pioneered a very similar set of ideas. Today these have been handed down to us as the Edicts of Ashoka. Legend has it that after a particularly brutal battle to expand his empire in central India, Ashoka was appalled by the carnage. He declared that from then on his kingdom would only fight defensive wars and carved a series of moral and cosmopolitan lessons inscribed publicly on huge pillars. These included injunctions to tolerate religious differences, to show compassions toward the suffering of other huma beings, and to dialog with other belief systems. Some authors like Jack Donnelly argue that these edicts might be considered the first real code of universal human rights; beating out the English Bill of Rights (1689) and the American Bill of Rights (1789-91) by almost 2000 years.

All this may seem very appealing on the surface; Diogenes' punk contempt for authority and Seneca's dignified egalitarianism both have had a long shelf life. But there is a darker side to the history of early cosmopolitanism that is considerably less admirable; one well traced by Martha Nussbaum in her recent book *Cosmopolitanism: A Noble but Flawed Tradition*. A tragic irony of the early tradition is that it is difficult to dissociate the history of cosmopolitanism from imperialism and political quietism on a lot of important issues. Diogenes may have been unafraid to tell Alexander the Great where to stick it, but Seneca, Marcus Aurelius and plenty of the other Stoics came from or rose to the heights of Roman nobility. They were admirable for wanting to gentle the rough edges of Roman imperialism but didn't go very far in questioning the legitimacy of the project as a whole. For a venerable statesman like Cicero, the divide between defending universal cosmopolitanism and the need to defend Rome's burgeoning Mediterranean hegemony would have been very thin indeed. More to the point, the Stoics were also noticeably silent about reforming the dramatically inegalitarian social and material conditions they saw around them. Rome had always been a slave society; an issue that came to the forefront of politics during the Servile Wars. Seneca argued that it was indeed wrong to mistreat the slaves but allowed that the institution of slavery itself may not be immoral. After all, the goodness of the soul was ultimately what mattered, and enslaving a person could not touch the dignity of the soul. Millenia later, Republican judges would justify the retention of homophobic policies on the same basis; that dignity was innate, and so inhibiting people from engaging in homosexual relations could in no way detract from their dignity.

These are topics to which we'll return many times. Cosmopolitanism has often had a radical edge to it that makes it eminently compatible with a tradition like socialism. Both are fundamentally humanistic doctrines that reject artificial differences in wealth and power playing a determinant role in social relations. But at many points cosmopolitanism can slide into a kind of cheesy moralism which sheds a tear for current social conditions but is incapable of getting at the real roots of the problem. At its worst cosmopolitanism can either serve as an apologetics or even a justification for the exercise of the most brutal forms of power; as Martti Koskeniemmi will remind us in *The Gentle Civilizer of Nations*, many of the Founding Fathers of international law saw colonialism as a way of spreading Enlightened doctrines across the world at the point of a gun. Wrestling with this legacy will be a major theme throughout this book. On the other hand, many forms of socialism that broke from the cosmopolitan spirit of the early movement to focus on the nation-state wound up also having a checkered record; sometimes a disastrous one. And arguably, in a post-globalization era, it is impossible to even think of a sincere socialism which isn't in some respects militantly cosmopolitan. More on that later.

The Origins of Just War Theory

Justice being taken away, then, what are kingdoms but great robberies? For what are robberies themselves, but little kingdoms? The band itself is made up of men; it is ruled by the authority of a prince, it is knit together by the pact of the confederacy; the booty is divided by the law agreed on. If, by the admittance of abandoned men, this evil increases to such a degree that it holds places, fixes abodes, takes possession of cities and subdues peoples, it assumes the more plainly the name of a kingdom, because the reality is now manifestly conferred on it, not by the removal of covetousness, but by the addition of impunity. Indeed, that was an apt and true reply which was given to Alexander the Great by a pirate who had been seized. For when that king had asked the man what he meant by keeping hostile possession of the sea, he answered with bold pride, "What you mean by seizing the whole earth; but because I do it with a petty ship, I am called a robber, while you who does it with a great fleet are styled emperor."

St Augustine, *City of God*

Beyond the cosmopolitan philosophies being developed by Diogenes, Ashoka and others there were modest efforts to codify and "gentle" the behavior of states. Ashoka's edicts were more than just moral wisdom; as the emperor he was able to give some teeth to his outlook. The Greeks held that the behavior of all peoples was to be determined not just by human but also natural laws, which included dictates on how other nations were to be treated in times of peace and war. Their conceptualization of natural law was predictably self-aggrandizing, and different rules applied to civilized (re Greek) and barbarian (mostly everyone else) peoples. But you have to start somewhere. Confucianism influenced generations of Chinese dynasties, with the concept of *Li* engendering respect for customs, ritual and diplomacy when interacting with others. Roman jurists spent a lot of time developing the concept of *jus gentium,* or the law of nations, which governed their interactions with other peoples. Many of the laws of nations concerned when states could permissibly go to war with one another, what was required to establish peace, and how to form alliances.

Each of these different traditions took a step toward trying to codify and give teeth to a fundamentally cosmopolitan ethos. But they were also undoubtedly self-serving and filled with loopholes that justified the strong mistreating the weak. So called civilized people – a quality always evaluated according to the standards of the beholder – were effectively justified in adopting a double standard toward the uncivilized. This included a prerogative to wage wars to spread the glories and virtues of civilization throughout the world.

One person who troubled this militaristic conceit was St Augustine of Hippo. As a young man Augustine traversed the declining Roman world, reflecting and developing his complex philosophical thoughts on time, humanity and God. He eventually settled on the Catholic faith of his mother, Monica, who had long hoped her beloved son would come to see the light. Augustine spent the remainder of his life developing arguably the first full philosophy of history, while offering commentaries and apologias on virtually every one of the Church's traditions and ideas. Modern Christianity and the cosmopolitan outlook owe a great deal to his writing, for better and for worse.

Augustine's concerns weren't purely theoretical. For 400 years the Roman Empire had kept the Mediterranean world more or less stable, bringing together hundreds of different peoples and faiths under imperial rule. But in 410 CE, the Visigoths under Alaric I sacked the eternal city, signaling to the whole world that the empire's decline was mortal. It's hard to comprehend the shock and fear this instilled in the millions of people who had come to depend on Rome. Many blamed Christianity for bringing about the empire's decline. For devotees of the old pagan gods, the lapse in faith was responsible for bringing about divine ruin. Of course, it's hard to take that seriously now. But a more subtle critique was leveled that Christianity and Christian universalism had led to Rome losing its martial edge. In the old days of Republican glory, the Romans were a proudly militaristic and aristocratic people, who deliberately sought out conflict and conquest. It was argued that the soft, egalitarian and compassionate doctrines of the Christians had led to these virtues rusting, leaving the empire open to attack by more vigorous and militant barbarians.

Augustine responded to this in *City of God* by developing what we now know as just war theory. He argued that, far from being glorious, the earlier Romans had been defined by the aforementioned libido domanandi. They sought power and glory for its own sake, giving into their sinful ambitions to rule over the mass of humankind to satiate their pride. In so doing they elevated the pursuit of power to the highest human ambition. But this in turn led to Rome's own downfall. Once the empire was established, it fell victim to countless civil wars and violence as a parade of General-Emperors, usurpers and petty tyrants competed with one another for the transient privilege of being the number one man in the empire. In so doing they squandered Rome's armies and riches, in addition to actively destroying the towns and infrastructure it had taken centuries to build. The sack of Rome itself had been prompted by the pretender emperor betraying his pledges to the Visigoths, who finally had enough of being treated like puppets in the factional games of the arrogant Romans.

There was a deeper point to these historical ruminations, which was that sinful behavior always begets destruction. Since humankind is defined by original sin, everything we try to build will eventually fall prey to the decay brought about by evil. The only way to overcome this was through God's love, which expressed itself in part through a series of moral lessons about what behaviors were good and what a just Christian society would look like. But here Augustine was faced with a problem. It had long been held to be God's will that, in the face of evil and violence, the good Christian must turn the other cheek. After all, Jesus allowed himself to be crucified by his enemies rather than fight back. But such a beatific attitude didn't seem like a good option in the face of the mounting barbarian invasions. If Christian society was to survive the fall of the Roman Empire, it would need to defend itself. So Augustine came to argue that Christians could indeed wage a just war under the right conditions and in the right manner. In the jargon of international humanitarian law, we say that one must ask whether we meet *jus ad bellum* and *jus in bello* conditions. *Jus ad bellum* refers to the conditions under which a just war might actually be fought. *Jus in bello* refers to the proper actions that must be taken within a war for it to be just.

Augustine deserves a lot of credit for these arguments, since he helped us think far more critically about what constitutes a just and unjust war. No longer would militant A-holes like "wise" Achilles get a pass just because they happened to be really good at killing people. Instead war and conflict had to be justified through appeal to universal moral principles. This was a big step forward in how to conceptualize a more pacific cosmopolitan order, and Augustine's formulations would precede further critical analyses into when war was permissible. Many of these wrestled with how one could rightly conflict with other human beings, given we are all God's children and are intended to live together as brothers and sisters. The Islamic philosopher Averroes wrote on why war should only be turned to as a last resort, since individuals and states should try to use persuasion and reason to resolve their problems instead. Maimonides forbade the use of wanton destruction during war, insisting that "one who smashes household goods, tears clothes, demolishes a building, stops up a spring, or destroys articles of food with destructive intent, transgresses the command 'You shall not destroy'".

The centrality of discussions of war to many religious philosophers may seem a bit narrow to contemporary cosmopolitans, who tend to have ambitions that go well beyond just preventing and humanizing the worst forms of conflict. But it is important to remember that at the time they wrote, peace was often an interruption of war and not the other way around. In his classic book *Just and Unjust Wars*, Michael Walzer points out that, then as now, adherents of the "war is hell" argument saw these efforts to humanize the most extreme conflicts as naïve. But they tend to lean heavily on a false bifurcation where we either have peace, or hellish war. I see no reason for this. One can still acknowledge war is hell while recognizing that an injunction not to bomb elementary schools might make it a bit less so. The fact that these early religious thinkers broached such an important issue testifies to both their originality and moral courage.

On the other hand, it is important not to oversell their passivity. Many of the reasons these religious philosophers gave for waging a just war would seem shocking, even fanatical, to us now. For instance, Augustine was right to argue that being peaceful in the face of evil would now be considered sinful. But what he considered evil was rather...broad. He insisted that Christians could rightly engage in a war if commanded to do so by divine injunction, which in practice meant when authorized by the Church or a Christian leader. Both tended to find this an expedient excuse to demand wars against the heathens to spread the true faith. This ethos sadly persisted well into the modern era, though it was often given different forms. The TWAIL (Third World Approaches to International Law) scholar Anthony Anghie has written extensively on how European states mobilized on behalf of a militant Christianity to invade and convert the heathens of North America. Analyzing the writings of Francisco de Vitoria, what Anghie shows is how the Europeans justified colonialism via the need to bring the true faith to the Mexica and other indigenous peoples. This overruled their rights to sovereignty and humane treatment, since in effect the Europeans were trying to save their immortal souls from eternal damnation. In the event that the original peoples of North America resisted proselytizing efforts, they could be put to the sword. Not exactly turning the other cheek...

This was not the last time a decent cosmopolitan principle

was adapted in a skewed and self-serving way. As we'll see, early liberals were more than happy to carve out exceptional arguments to justify the spread of capitalism across the globe.

Early Liberalism and Capitalism in Grotius, Hobbes and Locke

Someone reading a book on cosmopolitan socialism might be surprised it has taken us this long to get to discussing capitalism. To them I say learn to be a little more patient. One of the reasons it was important to get a sense of the earlier cosmopolitan tradition was to recognize both its strengths and weaknesses. Its universalism could take on very admirably humanitarian traits, from Ashoka's insistence on dialog over violence to Augustine's yearning to humanize war. But it could also quickly turn apolitical at best, and even serve as a justification for imperialism and violence at worst. For many Marxist theorists, these kinds of intellectual movements are emblematic of ideology, and these theorists are in many senses correct. The same will be true of possessive individualist strains of liberalism, which came to serve an ideological function in defending the spread of capitalism across the globe. By the barrel of a gun in many cases.

One of the emblematic features of early liberal cosmopolitan was its gradual effort to wean itself off of the naturalistic and mythological arguments of antiquity and the medieval era. This was hardly a straightforward process and plenty of classical and scholastic arguments persist in the writings of authors like Grotius, Hobbes and Locke. But what characterizes their work is a gradual belief that the universalistic moral outlook of the Stoics and the great religious traditions, could be grounded in human subjectivity and reason rather than any external source. This would have been incoherent for Aristotle, for whom universal natural law needed to be discovered in nature itself, or to Ibn Sinna, for whom the human intellect could gradually come

29

through "divine effluence" to recognize the activity of Allah in all existence. To this day, the most sophisticated opponents of the great modernist doctrines of liberalism and socialism gravitate to these kinds of arguments and strive mightily to prove that any effort to ground universalism in subjectivity is doomed to lead to nihilism in the long run.

Whether this is true or not is something we'll put aside here. The reason I bring it up is because liberal and cosmopolitan socialism will overlap a great deal in regarding these kinds of naturalistic and mythological arguments as both wrong and deeply embedded in the ideological defense of hierarchy and privilege. This is because the notion that there is some unchanging and ordered pattern to which all human beings must conform because nature or God demands it, seems a serious inhibition on both individuals' freedom and human equality. It often serves as a defense of established power by implying specifics and contingent forms of power are either natural or divinely sanctioned. Both liberals and later socialists will take issue with such a position. The biggest difference is that we socialists think that, while liberals were right to turn their barbs on naturalistic and mythological defenses of aristocratic hierarchy, they fell into the same trap when coming to defend capitalism and stratified private property relations. If it is true that men make their own history, it means that the belief that capitalism is inevitable and natural (as Locke seemed to think) is no truer than the claim that God wanted Louis XVI to have his ass glued to the throne of France.

The most important early liberal cosmopolitan was undoubtedly Hugo Grotius, who competes with Alberico Gentili for the title of "father of modern (European) international law." Grotius led a far more interesting life than his always dry, relentlessly scholarly books would imply. He was a public figure who contributed to many of the most important debates of his time about religious toleration and the use of war to spread doctrine. More than once his views got him into trouble, and he was even imprisoned in 1619. Fortunately, Grotius' wife loved him enough to help organize his escape in 1621. While he was living in exile in Paris, Grotius wrote and published his most important book, *On the Laws of War and Peace*, in 1625. This included a shocking claim that, even if God did not exist or at minimum didn't give a shit about what human beings did, the natural laws set forward in Grotius' book would still hold and could be recognized through reason. He was one of the first to argue that individuals possess fundamental rights in relation to the state, which emerged because individuals transferred powers to it for the protection of those rights and the maintenance of peace. Many of the rights he defended are admirable, including to individual autonomy and religious tolerance. Others are far less so. For instance, Grotius argued for a particularly weighty right to personal property that few socialists would accept. Even more problematically, he contended that slavery could be justified on the basis that people had a right to sell their labor and even their liberty to another. What we see beginning with him is the concept of the state as the willful creation of individuals seeking to protect their natural rights to autonomy, property and to live off the alienated labor of others. Grotius also universalized this liberal ideal through his cosmopolitan arguments about the law of nations, insisting that the arguments he was making held for all time and all peoples and could be apprehended through an individual's power of reasoning.

Grotius was responding to the emergence of what we now call the Westphalian international order, so named for the *Treaty of Westphalia* in 1648. Nominally a treaty to end the bloody Thirty Years War, the Westphalian ideal was of a world of separate states led by sovereign rulers whose control was uncontested within their jurisdiction. But whether uncontested meant absolute was obviously a big question that would come to define much of later European politics. For proto liberals like

Grotius, the sovereign still had a duty to respect the rights of his citizens. Most prominently to property. This will become more important as time goes on.

Building heavily on this framework was Thomas Hobbes: the most significant philosopher to ever write in the English language, as John Rawls put it. Hobbes lived during a particularly tumultuous century for Britain, as the relative peace and prosperity of the Elizabethan era gave way to religious and political agitation, civil war and the gradual ascendency of parliament over the monarchy. As a naturally cautious man, needless to say none of this was to Hobbes's liking. In his masterpiece *Leviathan,* he developed a complex argument for what (on the surface) appears to be an absolutist state. But Hobbes's reasoning was very different than the kind of scholastic patriarchal claims popular with other early modern defenders of absolutism. He argued that in a state of nature all human beings were very much equals, particularly intellectually. There was also no private property since that would require a state to enforce property entitlements. Instead each of us could only possess as much as we were able so long as we were able. This led to a competition for resources in the state of nature, leading to the infamous "warre of all against all" and resulting in an existence that was solitary, poor, nasty, brutish and short for most of us. Rather than put up with this, prudent individuals in a state of nature would wisely transfer their shared absolute right to all things into an exclusive right to some things, backed up by the sovereign state. As the legal theorist David Dyzenhaus reminds us, this sovereign state would not be quite as absolutist as some of Hobbes's critics contended. But it would be quite strong, and we'd have little reason to complain, since the alternative was a return to the state of nature.

Interestingly, the account of international relations developed circa Hobbesian thinking was stridently anti-cosmopolitan, but in an interesting way. You still see flavors of Hobbesian realism pop up in international relations theory semi-regularly. This is because Hobbes argued the sovereign had absolute control over all the land and people he effectively controlled. Beyond that there were other sovereigns who also held a monopoly on the legitimate use of force in other parts of the world. Between these sovereigns there could be no cosmopolitan order, since that would require them to submit to some higher authority (reason, international law, a proper conception of religion) than themselves. But Hobbes considered this absurd, and in fact spent a great deal of time attacking the Catholic Church and its followers for holding just such universalistic pretensions. There was no earthly authority above the sovereign, meaning that morally and legally all effective sovereigns confronted one another as equals. We already know how that ended up in the state of nature. Just as equal individuals war with one another in the state of nature, so to do sovereigns war among themselves for land, resources, and for protection. The way to understand the international realm is therefore neither like Stoics' well-ordered cosmos, or Grotius' law of nature. Instead the war of all against all continued on the international realm.

This is important when we try to understand the ideological justifications for liberal imperialism which were to emerge. While some liberals justified imperialism through appeal to the need to spread higher moral principles, Hobbesians were far more brutal. In *The Political Theory of Possessive Individualism* socialist political philosopher CB Macpherson argued that Hobbes was one of the first to reflect the ideological logic or emergent market society back to readers in his work. Macpherson's helpful label for this was that Hobbes, Locke and many of the other early liberals were beholden to an ideology of "possessive individualism." Hobbes' conception of human beings is as desire driven, prudent individualistic units who compete with one another until a higher power compels us to cooperate. One of the big reasons we're willing to put up with this higher power is the protection it offers to our property; first and foremost our life, but also our house, farm etc. With this accomplished domestically we can only give into this competitive and acquisitive urge through the mechanisms of the market. In this respect the market both pacifies and gives expression to our acquisitive nature and the aggression that induces. But even that isn't enough to satiate the most desirous among us, who will consequently turn to war and conquest as a way of gaining further riches, colonies and control. Macpherson argues that this was latent in Hobbes but became far more overt in Locke.

John Locke is a favorite author of many American conservatives, and it's not hard to see why. Few people were as vigorous in defending an ultra-expansive conception of private property as he was. Unlike Hobbes, who was arguably more brutally honest about the kind of individualism emerging in possessive individualist society, Locke preferred to present it in more genteel terms. In the *Second Treatise on Government*, Locke describes a state of nature where we are desire-driven and competitive, but not necessarily war like. Instead we seek to improve our lot through the one fundamental human power available to us: labor. Human beings mix their labor with the land around them in order to produce and accumulate goods, and in so doing gain a property entitlement to both the land and what they produce. Interestingly Locke expressly compares his own civilization, where differentiated applications of labor have created widely divergent property entitlements, to North America, which was apparently a *terra nullius* or unclaimed land. The implication was that the original peoples of North America were not entitled to the land they lived on, since Locke made the racist assumption that they simply didn't labor on it efficiently enough for the purposes of commerce to claim it as an entitlement. As he put it:

Where there is not some thing, both lasting and scarce, and so valuable to be hoarded up, there men will not be apt to enlarge their possessions of land, were it never so rich, never so free for them to take: for I ask, what would a man value ten thousand, or an hundred thousand acres of excellent land, ready cultivated, and well stocked too with cattle, in the middle of the inland parts of America, where he had no hopes of commerce with other parts of the world, to draw money to him by the sale of the product? It would not be worth the enclosing, and we should see him give up again to the wild common of nature, whatever was more than would supply the conveniences of life to be had there for him and his family. Thus in the beginning all the world was America, and more so than that is now; for no such thing as money was any where known. Find out something that hath the use and value of money amongst his neighbours, you shall see the same man will begin presently to enlarge his possessions.

Of course in the state of nature our natural right to what became our property was ineffectively enforced and subject to threat. Rather like with Hobbes, this is why we chose to band together to create a state; though in this case, one that will remain more representative so it can be responsive to the needs and interest of property owners. One of those needs was quite interesting. Locke acknowledged that once the land was entirely swallowed up, this would leave large swathes of the population with little opportunity to create their own property entitlements through mixing their labor with unclaimed matter. The only way for them to survive would therefore be to sell the one thing they had – their labor – to what we would later call capitalists who owned property, in return for a wage. After which the capitalist got to keep what their workers produced. This was an extremely telling turn. From labor being the source of all property entitlements, Locke's thinking moved to argue that whole swathes of people would need to alienate their labor for others but not be able to keep what it was they produced. To compel those disadvantaged by such a system to accept it, a strong state would be required. As Macpherson put it, referring to Locke's arguments:

To permit such a society to function, political authority must be supreme over individuals; for if it is not, there can be no assurance that the property institutions essential to this kind of individualism will have adequate sanctions. The individuals who have the means to realize their personalities (that is, the properties) do not need to reserve any rights as against civil society, since civil society is constructed by and for them, and run by and for them...The wholesale transfer of individual rights was necessary to get sufficient collective force for the protection of property. Locke could afford to propose it because the civil society was to be in control of the men of property. In these circumstances individualism must be, and could safely be, left to the collective supremacy of the state...It is not a question of the more thorough individualism, the less collectivism; rather the more thorough going the individualism, the more complete the collectivism.

With Locke, early liberal theory therefore had all the tools in place to justify a very peculiar international regime. It would be predicated on a universalistic set of beliefs, held to be transhistorical, emphasizing a possessive individualist vision of human beings as self-interested and competitive. In this sense it was deeply hostile to the aristocratic naturalisms and mythologies of the earlier era, which conceived of society as an organic whole where each person had their place. In many respects early liberalism had an emancipatory dimension. It liberated individuals from a hegemonic ideology which was hostile to the quasi-egalitarian ambitions of liberalism.

The early liberals believed that, at least in the beginning, we were all equal. It was through our labor and competition that inequalities emerged. Liberal societies would be dynamic, propulsive and defined by the creative destruction of the market. Liberal theory would also insist on both the need to create and maintain separate and powerful states to protect property rights from interference, while at the same time trying desperately to insulate the market from political pressures aimed at redistribution. This latter point became far more pressing as time went on, and democratic movements emerged – sometimes drawing on liberal theory, and sometimes hostile to it. Classical liberals like James Madison were willing to tolerate some forms of political participation by the propertied, which might be quasi-democratic. But they were not willing to allow the unpropertied the chance to use the state or any other mechanism to challenge what they took to be the justifiable inequities which emerged from market dynamics.

But here came the most noxious turn yet. The Westphalian division of the world into sovereign states, which offered protections for property rights, was held to apply to other "civilized" peoples. In theory this meant those who broadly embraced their conception of the world, and in practice it meant those who were powerful enough to resist the spearhead of European colonialism. The hypocrisy of this was quite obvious: how could an ideology focused on state sovereignty and the protection of individual rights justify not just empire building, but empire building on a hitherto unknown scale? The answer was very much a Lockean one. Those peoples who lacked the power to defeat European and American invasions were denigrated as uncivilized, not actually entitled to the land since they failed to labor on it effectively, and of course not really human and so not the bearer of human rights. In an American context the Founding Fathers would appeal to Lockean style arguments to justify invading the western part of the continent, denigrating the indigenous peoples as racially inferior and unable to use their land effectively. Thomas Jefferson spoke to the attitude when he was discussing conflict with the indigenous peoples in a letter to Alexander von Humboldt in 1813:

to teach them agriculture and the rudiments of the most necessary arts, and to encourage industry by establishing among them separate property. In this way they would have been enabled to subsist and multiply on a moderate scale of landed possession. They would have mixed their blood with ours and been amalgamated and identified with us within no distant period of time. On the commencement of our present war, we pressed on them the observance of peace and neutrality, but the interested and unprincipled policy of England has defeated all our labors for the salvation of these unfortunate people. They have seduced the greater part of the tribes within our neighborhood, to take up the hatchet against us, and the cruel massacres they have committed on the women and children of our frontiers taken by surprise, will oblige us now to pursue them to extermination.

So what emerged in the early liberal era was a strange mélange of emancipatory principles advocating universal human rights, a defense of the modern leviathan of state and its active role in advancing market culture, a wariness of that same state where it might prove a tool to challenge property, a defense of sovereignty for the "civilized" world of possessive individualism, and a limitless right to conquer and even exterminate those who were deemed uncivilized by European standards. A century-and-a-half later, Marx and Engel's would correctly diagnose the emergence of these ideological tensions as being a consequence of the complex dynamics of nascent capitalism, as the new ruling classes sought on the one hand to justify revolutionary emancipation from the aristocracy and on the other to deny equality to millions of others. The post-colonial scholar Edward Said will put it a different way and argue that European imperialism was defined by a complex dynamic of both asserting the universalism of its foundational principles while constructing an "Other" who failed to embody them. To early liberals, European and American men were rational, manly, industrious, and individualistic while their "Other" in the Orient and elsewhere was emotion, effeminate, lazy and communitarian. This justified colonialism on paternalistic lines, rather like those espoused by Jefferson, where in fact the job of Europeans and Americans was to bring civilization to those who lacked it. This was Rudyard Kipling's infamous "white man's burden."

Saying that, we shouldn't underestimate the capacity of many liberals to become critical of hypocritical geopolitics. One such liberal was Immanuel Kant.

Immanuel Kant and Liberal Cosmopolitanism

Kant's influence on the history of cosmopolitan thinking can hardly be overstated; indeed for some international lawyers even talking about Kantian cosmopolitanism is oxymoronic. No doubt this venerable status may be surprising to those who are only familiar with Kant's ultra-dry, technical transcendental philosophy which seems leagues removed from the worldly concerns cosmopolitanism seeks to address. But in fact there is a deep link between his eminently modernist philosophy and the kind of arguments many of us – including plenty of people on the left – make for the cosmopolitan outlook. Kant's thinking is also important since he exposes a more admirable side to liberal universalism than what we saw with Grotius, Hobbes and Locke. In this respect he can help us understand what parts of the liberal tradition are worth preserving in cosmopolitan socialism.

At the heart of Kant's project as a whole was his practice

of critique. This word is thrown around an awful lot; go to any academic bookstore and you'll find critiques of political economy, critiques of everyday life, critiques of post-colonial, instrumental and pure reason, and pretty much everything else under the sun. Kant inarguably was the most important figure in engendering this shift. For Kant, critique is about more than just criticism. Mere criticism rests easy with pointing out the contradictions, false claims and bad outcomes produced by a viewpoint. Critique instead tries to explain not just what is wrong with a position, but the conditions under which it emerged. For example, the critique of political economy inaugurated by Marx isn't just a series of criticisms leveled against contemporary capitalism. Instead Marxism seeks to explain the historical laws of motion which brought about capitalism in the first place, describes the kind of ruling ideologies which emerge to justify it, and analyzes the various ways in which capitalism might stabilize itself or ultimately fall apart. The critique of political economy also demonstrates the limitations inherent to capitalism which render it unable to fully resolve its fundamental contradictions.

Kant's initial project was aimed at explaining how pure reason was possible for human subjects, before going on to explore its fundamental limitations in terms of what we can possibly know. As it turned out these limitations are quite glaring; Kant insists that from the standpoint of pure reason at least, we'll never have an answer to big questions about the transcendent meaning of existence. These include whether there is a God, if the universe had a beginning within time and so on. But this became morally and politically problematic because so many of us believe that we can discover a permanent answer to the questions of where transcendent meaning arises. Reactionaries are especially prone to this conceit. They insist that we must believe in a source of sublime transcendent meaning in order to stabilize our convictions about existence, and to accept the role we are to play within it. For instance, the conservative Catholic Church of Kant's era saw is role as providing ideological support for the maintenance of the French monarchy. It did this in part through implying it was part of God's plan for the French state to be organized in the hierarchical form it assumed. Conservatives have often continued making these kinds of arguments down to the present day, often posturing as having some transcendent wisdom which goes beyond the banalities available to mere self-interested materialism. The alt-right converts of contemporary "traditionalism" ala Alexander Dugin et al are a good example. Though somehow, the profound God of conservativism, in all his transcendence, remains concerned with some rather mundane things. Surprisingly these include a lot of the concerns of well-off white dudes in late middle age: where his creation chooses to stick their genitals, how annoying campus activists are, and of course the fact that kids these days won't stay the hell off people's lawns. Some mysteries are simply too deep for us to grasp of course.

But Kant insisted that this was nonsensical since the project of critique had shown there was no way to know God's will in the way defenders of absolutism claimed. So when they claimed to have access to a transcendent insight that revealed how things must be, they were in fact merely giving an ideological expression to either their own preferences or those of the heteronymous society they were part of. This constituted a failure to think for themselves, which Kant eventually came to believe should be the fundamental mantra of the burgeoning Enlightenment. Moreover when we shed ourselves of the illusion that meaning comes from a transcendent source, Kant came to believe our freedom was enhanced. Rather than receiving normativity from outside ourselves, each individual was required to be a moral law giver in themselves, with the only limitation being the dictates of their own practical reason willing the moral law.

This all came to a head during the French Revolution, which

Kant embraced with qualifications. Being somewhat personally conservative but politically a liberal republican, he supported the efforts to break down monarchial rule while being reserved about the breakdown of law and order and the advent of revolutionary violence. But one of the interesting features of his response was Kant's tremendous enthuses for universalizing the republican and liberal principles of the revolutionary era. This meant they needed to be gradually detached from the nationalist rhetoric and militarism increasingly associated with the period, and which would culminate in republican France transitioning to the First French Empire under Napoleon I. To this effect Kant produced several important works of political theory arguing for republican government, including *The Metaphysics of Morals*. But he also wrote most of the essays which inaugurated the tradition of Kantian cosmopolitanism, which a century-and-a-half later had its moment in the sun in the aftermath of the Second World War.

By far the most significant of these was Kant's 1795 essay "Toward Perpetual Peace: A Philosophical Sketch." It's not a long essay – maybe 20 pages in most English translations – but it is staggeringly ambitious. Kant argues that the competitive drive for power and wealth that characterized Europe through the eighteenth century is a very great evil. Allowing the Hobbesian warre of all against all to carry on between the nations has led to untold death and suffering. Much of this is further propelled by the persistence of feudalism and absolutism. Because the rulers of many states owe squat to their citizens but still demand obedience, they see nothing wrong with sending hundreds of thousands of their fellow men to die so the Bourbon family can acquire yet another dutchy east of the Rhine. Consequently Kant argues that all states must transition toward a republican form of government, that such states should band together in a federation, and gradually seek to both eliminate armies and make war permanently illegal. As he put it:

The only constitution which has its origin in the idea of the original contract, upon which the lawful legislation of every nation must be based, is the republican. It is a constitution, in the first place founded in accordance with the principle of the freedom of the members of society as human beings: secondly, in accordance with the principle of the dependence of all, as subjects, on a common legislation: and, thirdly, in accordance with the law of the equality of the members as citizens. It is then, looking at the question of right, the only constitution whose fundamental principles lie at the basis of every form of civil constitution. And the only question for us now is, whether it is also the one constitution which can lead to perpetual peace. Now the republican constitution apart from the soundness of its origin, since it arose from the pure source of the concept of right, has also the prospect of attaining the desired result, namely, perpetual peace. And the reason is this. If, as must be so under this constitution, the consent of the subjects is required to determine whether there shall be war or not, nothing is more natural than that they should weigh the matter well, before undertaking such a bad business. For in decreeing war, they would of necessity be resolving to bring down the miseries of war upon their country.

This was also complemented by further calls which were quite radical for the time. Kant argued for what is arguably the word's first refugee rights, saying that those fleeing war and hardship had a right to "universal hospitality" wherever they went. He was also increasingly critical of the European colonial system, arguing it constituted an unjustifiable breach of other people's sovereignty. This certainly didn't mean Kant suddenly became woke by twenty-first century standards, and to the end he held to many of the xenophobic and racist views of his day. Critical race and post-colonial scholars like Gayatri Spivak, in her *Critique of Postcolonial Reason*, have launched well-deserved attacks on his pathetic anthropological ruminations – all done second hand – which contained a great deal of cringeworthy comments about the mental infantilism of lesser cultures. This is not an idle point either, since of course much of Kant's sunny ruminations about Enlightenment are tied to his historical beliefs that it constitutes humanity's emergence from a self-incurred immaturity. His belief that many non-European peoples simply hadn't reached this point yet was a supreme form of arrogance. Its contemporary descendants include many members of the intellectual dark web that Michael Brooks so effectively criticized in *Against the Web*. But on the other hand, it is important to recognize Kant's arguments that, in spite of their inferiority, Europeans were not entitled to simply invade and colonize others under the auspices of spreading the civilization was relatively progressive and far sighted for its time. Too many of his justifications for this position turn on the damage competition for colonies and glory causes to the European concert of geopolitics, and many of us would prefer him to have been more strident in insisting that colonialism was simply wrong in itself. But he was right that this competition would continue to drag European states into war with one another, culminating with the apex of imperialist competition during the horrific First World War. Kant was also correct that a global order of democracies was less likely to go to war with one another; what we now call democratic peace theory.

Kant's vision of a humanitarian, pacific and liberal republican cosmopolitanism seemed quaint at the time. During the nineteenth century there were indeed anti-aristocratic revolutions that began to topple the old order, but they were quickly replaced with gloves-off capitalist regimes that were nearly as hierarchical and certainly just as warlike. Efforts to humanize the international order through the founding of institutions like the Red Cross, and to moderate warfare through the *Hague Conventions*, expressed an admirable side to the kind of rights-respecting liberalism that Kant endorsed. But generally speaking it was not cosmopolitanism but nationalism and imperialism which were the order of the day. In his critique of Kant's cosmopolitan project, Hegel argued that the stalwart Prussian had failed to recognize that our sense of ethical obligations was invariably derived from more local attachments. Most of us will always feel a greater sense of obligation to those who are close to us, or more worryingly "like" us, than the "other." Consequently – according to the more conservative Hegel of the *Philosophy of Right* at least – the highest form of legal order that was sustainable was the nation-state. Any aspiration to found a more formal cosmopolitan order of the kind Kant longed for was doomed to run up against the limitations of our ethical imaginations. Until at least 1945, most respectable liberal and conservative commentators tended to think Hegel was spot on. Indeed to the extent they thought a cosmopolitan order was possible, it would be one of European empire's spreading themselves around the globe while carrying on just the kind of competitions Kant so disdained. Indeed the efforts of many international lawyers were directed precisely at legitimating and formalizing this project. Usually this was accompanied by racist narratives of "modernization" or bringing modernity to the decadent other. As the international lawyer Martti Koskeniemmi put it in his seminal book *The Gentle Civilizer of Nations: The Rise and Fall of International Law 1870-1960*:

despite occasional disagreement about particular geographical disputes or doctrinal matters such as the conditions of effective occupation, the effect of native treaties or the legal position of colonial companies, international lawyers shared a sense of the inevitability of the modernizing [re colonizing] process.

Early Socialism and Internationalism

One group that was determined to disprove this point were the early international socialist movements, many of them profoundly inspired by Marx's own critical inversion of the Hegelian project. The young Marx famously launched his own *Critique of Hegel's Philosophy of Right* early on, arguing that the kind of ethical harmonization between nation and state carried out by right-wing Hegelians was woefully wrongheaded. Hegel's conservative followers effectively reinscribed irrationalist and romantic ideas about identity into his account of the state in order to harmonize actually existent conflicts through a system of idealism. In this account the tensions that exist in life were to be resolved through recognizing the fundamental equivalence of our identity and interests with others who shared our ethnicity. These were both managed and instantiated through the state and its institutions, including state-managed hierarchies, which reflected the expression of our identity in rational historical form. As the most rational political form, any conflicts that would persist should take place between nation-states rather than within them.

Marx ridiculed this as naïve idealism. The bourgeois state which was emerging in the nineteenth century aspired to a unity of national identity and institutions which could only ever be achieved in thought because it missed the far more subtle and dramatic material transitions that were actually appearing on the ground. This was the transition from the feudal mode of production, which had similarly relied on a kind of scholastic idealism to justify itself, to the capitalist mode of production. In these circumstances, much as how the bourgeois liberal class eventually came into conflict with the old feudal order, the interests of the laboring masses would inexorably come into conflict with those of the new ruling class. Moreover, the capitalist mode of production itself would be fundamentally constrained by its own immanent contradictions, which would lead to destabilization over the long run. In fact the job of the modern state, according to Marx, was not to achieve the kind of harmony between identity and institutions longed for by Hegelian idealists. It was to manage the inexorable conflicts that would emerge from the tensions and contradictions brought about by the capitalist mode of production.

Capitalist ideology tried to avoid this problem through either naturalizing or mythologizing capitalist political economy, thereby stripping it of its historical particularity and seemingly placing it beyond the corrosion of time. In the nineteenth century, more forward-thinking liberals tended to favor the naturalization offered by the latest flavors of possessive individualism; Herbert Spencer's social Darwinism and Malthus' gloom economics of starvation, for example. These held that the emergent hierarchies that appeared both within capitalist societies, and between the advanced states and their colonies, were the inevitable and natural result of differences in ability and drive. Even an often-praiseworthy liberal socialist like JS Mill could fall into this temptation as when he infantilized the people of India through justifying colonialism. More right-wing liberals and outright reactionaries leaned more heavily on the kinds of traditionalist mythologizations offered by Carlyle, de Maistre, and, of course, right-Hegelianism. Oftentimes, particularly in a continental context, these flirted or embraced outright illiberalism and sought the restoration of the pre-capitalist order. None were entirely successful in this regard, since as Marx and Engels pointed out the productive power of capitalism was such that no state could afford to ignore its innovations without being rapidly outclassed by emerging industrial powerhouses. But these mythologizations put forward that the anti-hierarchical spirit of both the most radical liberals and emergent socialists constituted a profound leveling of the highest ideals, whose climax would be decadent vulgarity at best and nihilism at worst. While these more reactionary figures tended to despise liberalism almost as much as socialism, they could make temporary alliances with those liberals who naturalized hierarchy since at least this offered some protections to existent property rights.

In classical Marxist accounts, though, there is more disagreement on this now, the argument ran that one or another of these problems would eventually lead to the revolutionary transition from the capitalist to the socialist and then communist modes of production. Capitalist and reactionary ideology would try to obscure this wherever possible, but in the end the veil would be lifted, and the expropriators would be expropriated. Marx's mature theory, as presented in *Capital* most prominently, gave a truly epic account of all these problems that remained unfinished at the time of his death. But there remain undeniable ambiguities. At what point the tension between the interests of labor and liberal capitalists would become sufficiently sharp, when the working classes transition from being a class "in itself" to a class "for itself" as Marx would say, and lead to revolution, Marx did not say. Nor was it clear which of the immanent contradictions of capitalism would prove the most fatal, or if capital would be able to respond to them successfully. In his book *Seventeen Contradictions and the End of Capitalism* the Marxist geographer David Harvey discusses...seventeen contradictions that have beset capitalism from the beginning. Some of these have proven a more existential threat than others, and Harvey contends that some which have been ignored – particularly with regard to the environment – are going to become more dangerous over time. But so far none has proven so damaging as to provoke the long-awaited dialectical transition.

Nevertheless, Marxism and other socialist movements did prove very influential in agitating for a kind of internationalist solidarity which transcended the nation-state system Hegel and others wanted so badly to uphold. They did so by pointing out that the material interest workers of all countries had in emancipation from global capitalism was far more significant than the idealist and ideological ethno-cultural, religious and nationalist differences foregrounded by conservatives. The Second International was founded in 1889 to foster cooperation between the emerging socialist parties of Europe, and to foster a sense that the liberation of workers in each country was a precondition for the liberation of workers in all countries. It had considerable success in compelling many capitalist states to enact modest reforms to redistribute wealth, shorten the work week and day, and even provide some public goods. Even Bismark's German empire felt the pressure; though socialist parties were banned through the 1890s the Iron Chancellor was compelled to institute some of the first welfare programs in history to stave off destabilizing agitation. Unfortunately these limited but important successes weren't enough to prevent the First World War, which was a crucial moment for early international socialism. There were some who called for a general workers strike, arguing that labor in all the capitalist countries shouldn't allow itself to be divided along immaterial nationalist lines. These calls went unheeded, and millions of working-class soldiers did their best to kill each other between 1914 and 1918.

This was a worrying sign that the vulgar Marxist conviction that material interests would inevitably transcend national identity and lead to an international uprising against capital was wrongheaded. It turned out that for many people the *volk* did indeed matter more than class. The problems of socialist internationalism were compounded in the aftermath of the Bolshevik revolution. While it initially looked like this might spark sympathetic and complementary uprisings elsewhere, it was not to be, and the Soviet Union quickly became a pariah and then totalitarian state trying to build "socialism in one country" under Stalin's icy gaze. Then came the rise of fascism in Italy and Germany, which seemed to many people to prove the transcendent value of nationalism would always supersede the materiality of international workers' interests. Though the fascists were eventually defeated in the Second World War, these lessons would be hard pills to swallow for socialist internationalism for decades.

Welfarism, Anti-Colonialism and Twentieth-Century Cosmopolitanism

The end of the Second World War was characterized by an intense degree of self-reflection and no little hypocrisy. On the one hand, many of the victorious states emerged determined to secure their independence and were under intense pressure to secure a new and better life for their citizens. Workers groups had remained organized and active through the war, and catalyzed the most sweeping efforts at achieving equality ever seen. William Beveridge's pioneering 1942 report calling for the British state to provide comprehensive welfare for all, followed by the Labour government of Clement Atlee creating the NHS (to this day Britain's most beloved institution), captured the spirit of the times. On the other hand, none of the Allies were particularly keen on eliminating their globe-spanning empires; indeed both the Soviet Union and the United States rapidly expanded their spheres of influence into eastern and western Europe and east Asia particularly. Critics like Gandhi and Ho Chi Minh quickly became disillusioned that the European's fight against Nazi and Japanese imperialism meant they had any intention of dismantling their own empires, and in fact the United States provided aid to enable the French to (temporarily) re-establish colonial rule in southeast Asia. Consequently there would be decades of struggle, much of it violent, as the colonized aspired to throw out the colonizer. An era of post-colonial nationalism set in, with many coming to see it as a long-awaited response to the tyrannical universalism of European colonialism. In many ways the post-modern turn toward militant particularism and against both liberalism and Marxism – two modernist doctrines par excellence – owes much to this time period.

Attempting to manage these conflicting dynamics was a new kind of cosmopolitan order, focused around internationalist efforts to codify universal normative standards for all states and hold accountable those who violated them. It owed a great deal to the Kantian project of imposing limitations on the excesses of state power in the international arena, though what counted as excesses and what one should do about them remained extremely controversial through the Cold War and indeed to this day. One of the paradigmatic accomplishments of the new cosmopolitan order were the Nuremberg and Tokyo tribunals, where the former leaders of the Axis powers were put on trial for crimes against peace, war crimes and, most notably, crimes against humanity. Later the Polish lawyer Raphael Lemke would coin the term genocide, from the Greek genos (meaning family or race) and the Latin cide (meaning killing), to try and account for the horrors of the gas chambers. Later, Lemke's innovation would be recognized in the *Genocide Convention* of 1948 – the first human rights treaty unanimously adopted by the United Nations. This was seen as a high-water moment for Kantian cosmopolitans, since it was intended to demonstrate that even the senior officials of a sovereign state could be held accountable under international law. This indicated that maintaining sovereign legitimacy was now conditional on respect for human rights. Since then both the trial of the Axis powers and later the entire effort to criminalize certain kinds of state action would be criticized as a form of victor's justice, or as yet another imposition of Western values on the Third World. But there was undoubtedly something important and progressive in the effort to give teeth to restrictions on state violence, and of course to widely condemn the evils of fascist totalitarianism as something beyond the pale. Indeed it represented a historical milestone of sorts if we think back to Ashoka and St Augustine and their efforts to humanize and limit the evils of war.

But the new cosmopolitans had ambitions that went far beyond just curbing the worst excesses of state violence. Many thought it would be possible to initiate a new era of global solidarity and peace through creating international institutions and formalizing a more ambitious and expansive conception of human rights that incorporated the emerging welfarist ideals. The United Nations was built upon the ashes of the failed League of Nations, and was given a little (not that that's saying much) more power to implement effective global policy. In 1948, 58 UN member states voted to adopt the *Universal Declaration of Human Rights,* which, while non-binding, remains the most frequent normative touchstone for many liberal and left-liberal cosmopolitans. Interestingly it included recognition of many economic and social rights which socialists could readily get behind. This included rights to healthcare, social security, to join trade unions, and to leisure. For this we owe a debt to Eleanor Roosevelt, who stepped out of the shadow of her late husband to pioneer a more generous conception of rights than conventional liberals were willing to offer. To this day the exact rights stipulated in the *Declaration* remain controversial; both in terms of their content, and the justification for them. The exact list was the product of extensive deliberation, and at its conclusion the French philosopher and Christian Democrat Jacques Maritain famously said they all agreed on what rights to include provided "no one asked us why." For some, the rights flowed from a humanistic commitment to moral equality and material well-being. For others, they were grounded in a specific faith tradition.

By the 1960s the UN had introduced the even more ambitious international *Covenants* on human rights. These were divided into two, with the Soviet Union and its allies championing the *International Covenant on Economic, Social and Cultural Rights* and the Western allies showing more love toward the

International Covenant on Civil and Political Rights. Unlike the UDHR, the two covenants were intended to be legally binding on all states. The IESCR included a long list of social rights, and most interesting a right to self-determination on the part of all peoples. This demonstrated the degree to which anti- and post-colonial commitments had become part of the global discourse, though how to frame self-determination remains irredeemably contentious. The ICCPR codified many of the standard liberal rights to association, political participation, religious liberty and so on. But interestingly it was one of, if not the, first major liberal documents to not include an express right to private property. This was a startling move away from possessive individualist iterations of liberalism and shows how far in an egalitarian direction many liberal states had moved by the 1960s.

How to go about achieving this was of course very ambiguous. For the most part it was interpreted as an injunction for individual nation-states to provide welfare for their respective citizens. But a few savvy commentators pointed out that this imposed a terrific burden on post-colonial states, which lacked the resources of France and the United Kingdom. In *The Wretched of the Earth*, Franz Fanon famously attacked the hypocrisy of the colonizer by pointing out that the high levels of development in the "West" – often taken as a sign of a higher level of civilizational and cultural accomplishment – were in no small part the result of exploiting the labor and resources of the developing world. From there it was not hard to infer that maybe the former imperial regimes had an obligation to assist their former colonies. In his influential paper "Famine, Affluence, and Morality," utilitarian philosopher Peter Singer expressed a related point in a drier way. He pointed out that since we can all agree that needless death and suffering are bad, we have an obligation to prevent it where doing so doesn't impose undue burdens on ourselves. This was captured by the drowning child thought experiment, where he asks us to imagine driving by a shallow pond where we see a child flailing in the water. We get out and realize we can save the child, but at the cost of an expensive pair of shoes we are wearing. Singer points out that most of us would be horrified by a choice not to save the child. Yet advanced Western countries and their citizens make a similar kind of choice every day by choosing to prioritize high levels of consumption over providing basic aid to the world's poorest. The power of these kinds of moral and historical objections led some in the 1970s to expect international law to require wealthy states to provide aid to, or even attempt to establish material equality with, the developing world.

Alas it was not to be, and the drift was always only ever partial. By the 1980s the neoliberal regimes of Reagan and Thatcher were in power, and the Cold War was heating up again. They would quickly turn the cosmopolitan project in a far more reactionary direction. To this day many progressive cosmopolitans remain nostalgic for this time period, with Jurgen Habermas lamenting the "unfinished project" of international modernization it reflected. More cynical critics point out that even the more modest ambitious of progressive cosmopolitans to limit the worst excesses of state violence were only ever partially fulfilled. Not to mention they were only effectively enforced in post-colonial states that had entered a tumultuous period after throwing out Western and Soviet hegemons: Yugoslavia, Cambodia, sub-Saharan Africa. The most expansive yearnings to create a cosmopolitan order that would implement welfarist reforms from on high, or at least compel all nation-states to do so, was never anything more than a utopian ideal. As Samuel Moyn points out in his book *Not Enough*, "welfare world" never really advanced much further than the schemas of well-meaning and intelligent but largely marginal left-liberal academics. At the best of times it was only the presence of strong and potentially threatening socialist movements in the advanced Western states that compelled capital to offer egalitarian concessions to domestic citizens. There was little or no interest in going beyond that, and as neoliberalism became globally hegemonic the moral emphasis shifted from equality and even high levels of welfare to merely providing a bare minimum for people to survive. It's to this issue that I'll now turn.

Chapter Two

Neoliberal Internationalism

Making the World Safe for Capitalism Again

Capitalism has always been a restless system, ever seeking new markets, commodities and innovation. Consequently it has always been global in its impact and ambition. This was noted most vividly by Marx and Engels, where they prophetically described the cosmopolitan sweep of capitalism in *The Communist Manifesto:* "The need of a constantly expanding market for its products chases the bourgeoisie over the entire surface of the globe. It must nestle everywhere, settle everywhere, establish connections everywhere. The bourgeoisie has through its exploitation of the world market given a cosmopolitan character to production and consumption in every country."

During the high period of European and American empire, the most dramatic manifestations of this cosmopolitan tendency were imperialism and colonialism. Many of the European colonies were transformed into vast reserves of cheap labor involved in the production of resources and simple consumer goods, mostly oriented around the economic needs of the mother country. Imperial projects were also directly justified as a way of occupying the ambitious and restless youth of Europe, who might otherwise direct their energies to reforming the domestic situation. In the colonies themselves elite youth were often raised in the model of the colonizer and encouraged to adopt Western value systems which stressed hard work, industrial innovation and the maintenance of order as paramount virtues. In the aftermath of the Second World War this contributed a great deal to the relatively pacific transition from empire to national self-determination, as it became clear that colonial elites would ensure their countries continued to play the same role in the global economy as before.

And to this day there are substantial hangovers from the colonial system. In his book *The Ethics of Trade and Aid*, Christopher D. Wraight points out how, despite being nominally committed to "free trade," the European Union in fact deploys a variety of protectionist policies to inhibit the sale of refined commodities from other countries. It hedges its market power to ensure that the products it receives are primarily raw resources, which domestic manufacturers will later refine and sell at a higher price. The consequence is that many former European colonies struggle to develop more sophisticated industries aimed at the production of refined commodities, since the market for them is comparatively limited. In effect the old system persists, but in a new guise.

Nevertheless there was a time when it appeared things might genuinely change. Through the mid-twentieth century, socialism was at the height of its prestige and even the major capitalist states were in the midst of transitioning to a welfarist model that would guarantee a relatively high quality of life to all. Many of the new nation-states to emerge from the rubble of European imperialism were keen to emulate this model in their own countries, and the constitutions of India, China, Egypt and elsewhere included substantial commitments to economic and social rights and even cooperative ownership. These echoed many of the aforementioned provisions for economic, social and cultural rights at the international level. Socialism was appealing to many of the emergent countries for a number of reasons. Firstly, the Soviet Union was seen as far less implicated in the project of global imperialism initiated by the major capitalist states. Developing countries could also typically count on at least some form of aid if they adopted elements of the Soviet model. Secondly, national self-determination was deeply tied to the conviction that a strong state was needed to both secure independence and construct governing and public institutions. The ideology of a weak or thin state simply didn't appeal in these contexts. Interestingly this applied even to those emergent countries which veered in a more capitalist direction, with Singapore, Korea, South Africa and elsewhere all blending capitalist markets with everything from soft authoritarianism to apartheid. And thirdly, socialism appealed to the egalitarian atmosphere of the time. People in the former colonies were angered at being treated as the "other" or inferior to the peoples of Europe and the United States for centuries. In such a context, many saw independence movements as an opportunity to achieve not simply (comparable) equality between peoples but within society. This often included eliminating the stratified ethnic hierarchies entrenched by the colonizers to help maintain control; sometimes with inspiring results as with South Africa, and sometimes disastrously as with Rwanda.

There were some impressive accomplishments initiated by these regimes. The Congress party under Jawaharlal Nehru faced truly epic challenges after India became independent, including a war with Pakistan, staggering inequality as a result of everything from the caste system to the British raj, and the aftermath of a major famine in Bengal. It quickly constructed the world's largest democracy, rapidly industrialized major regions of the country, and instituted long-needed reforms in education. He was the first to institute compulsory primary education for all in India; though the sheer scale of the country and regional disparities have meant it has taken decades for that to be implemented in a truly egalitarian fashion. If Gandhi was the spiritual father of Indian independence, Nehru was undoubtedly its godfather and much of the longevity of Indian democracy and its gradual shift toward a tech-economy is owed to his efforts. In the 1990s, when apartheid finally ended in South Africa and the African National Congress took over there were a swathe of redistributive efforts to try and end the legacy of the racial divide. These included securing parity on education, trying to build new homes, and controversial land redistribution policies. But it is important to recognize that many of the socialist (and capitalist) regimes that emerged were hardly perfect and many were outright disasters. The Maoist effort to collective agriculture through the "Great Leap Forward" was just as disastrous as the Soviet one, resulting in the largest famine in human history and a doubling down on authoritarianism. Robert Mugabe in Zimbabwe was initially a well-known anti-colonial hero to many on the left, and he was indeed instrumental in attacking racial policies privileging the white minority. But in office Mugabe quickly instituted many disastrous kleptocratic policies servicing himself and engaged in reckless financial policies that led to hyperinflation and impoverishment. Leftists looking back at this period need to acknowledge these problems and learn from them.

But at the time, to many defenders of capital, these developments looked like an absolute disaster. The more liberal tended to accept that European empire was unstable, unjust and probably doomed to failure from the get-go. But it did inadvertently help create vast swathes of open markets that look set to erode under pressure from post-colonial statism. And provide a bulwark against the appeals of socialism. One of the primary ambitions of the neoliberals would be to try and recreate imperial conditions in a context where empire was now out of fashion.

The Sublime Market

It cannot be denied that Fascism and similar movements aiming at the establishment of dictatorships are full of the best intentions and that their intervention has, for the moment, saved European civilization. The merit that Fascism has thereby won for itself will live on eternally in history.
Ludwig von Mises, Liberalism

Neoliberalism can be defined as a mode of governance that aims to encase the market from political pressures; particularly those that emerge in democratic societies. This was of course one of the major ambitions of right-wing liberals and many conservatives from the beginning of the modern era onwards. Right-wing liberals supported the expansion of the state where necessary to complement the ambitions of the market and lamented its extension where that posed a threat to private property and its privileges. This included establishing the complex set of laws and associated punishments which far outstripped the simple penal codes of antiquity, building school and technical institutions to ensure the domestic labor force was capable of competing in the globalizing market, and of course constructing the architecture of parliamentary deliberation. But what made neoliberalism distinctive was a recognition, in the aftermath of the welfarist reforms of the mid-twentieth century, that the left had indeed learned how to both capture state power and exercise it to redistribute wealth through public services and potentially even challenge property rights. This was tremendously alarming, and neoliberals from von Mises to Hayek had a bad habit of throwing in their lot with the most reactionary and authoritarian movements where they worked to undermine these progressive efforts. However, it was their remarkably ambitious intention to create a global network of international laws, regulations and disciplinary institutions that was profoundly novel.

Before I go on it is important to recognize the way neoliberal theorists conceived of the market, since that is central to grasping their international ambitions. Classical political economists from Adam Smith onward were very much inspired by the Enlightenment's quest for certainty, which could be seen in their efforts to fully comprehend the dynamics of the market. Indeed the theoretical sweep of their work testified to just how ambitious they truly were on this point. Adam Smith's *The Wealth of Nations* is panoramic in scope, discussing the interactions of everything from the industrial division of labor to the impact of mercantilist policies, the dangers of monopolization, and the evils of emergent crony capitalism. The works of Malthus, Mill and David Ricardo are filled with complex logical arguments about iron laws of productivity, value and distribution. And, of course, Marx's epochal achievement was to integrate the whole idea of political economy into the dialectical "science of history." But what was problematic about these ambitions from a neoliberal standpoint is that they held out the possibility of being able to fully grasp the nature of the economy. If that were possible, not only would we be able to make certain predications about its operations but we could potentially even guide them through direct action. The epistemic optimism of classical and neoclassical political economy was a necessary precursor to both the utopianism of the early socialists, the harder edged historicism of the Marxists, and even the sweeping statism of Keynesian macroeconomy analysis.

The latter is an especially important foe for neoliberals, since it was the most technically sophisticated and in-vogue economic theory which held out the possibility of the state directly intervening in the market for humanist purposes. Keynes himself was by no means a radical; coming from an elite background he was more than a little haughty in his disdain for the ordinary and boring people. His argument for macro-economic theory and state intervention had more to do with lifting capitalism out of crisis through temporary statist measures aimed at raising employment and so boosting consumer spending. This would in turn incentivize capitalists to reinvest and essentially restart the depressed economy. But the many Keynesians who followed were far more ambitious than the master. In books like *The Affluent Society*, John Kenneth Galbraith postulated that one could employ statist tools to effectively create a social democratic society where at least the basic needs of all were cared for. This could be done so long as we bucked the conventional wisdom that economics was simply an impenetrable discipline too removed for public officials and citizens to grasp.

For the neoliberals, all of this was exceptionally dangerous thinking. The conceit that we could understand the market was the first brick on the road to hell since it paved the way for thinking we can and should control it. This was a deep error. Early in his career FA Hayek was a relatively conventional empiricist, who criticized state intervention in things like the volume of money on the basis that officials simply didn't know the evidence about inflationary cycles. But as time went on, he and his fellows came to adopt a far more interesting perspective, well described by Quinn Slobodian in his book *Globalists: The End of Empire and the Birth of Neoliberalism*. This was that the economy was something akin to a Kantian sublime object or process. It was a near infinitely vast and complex network of information sharing, with prices sending signals to consumers who responded through either consumption or saving, which had evolved organically over time through a quasi-Darwinian process and which was well adapted to servicing human needs. At any given part of the global economy we could potentially understand a little bit about what was going on. But understanding the totality of the interrelated global economy for even a moment, let alone the dynamics of market processes over time, was impossible.

Nevertheless, this didn't prevent well-meaning but often arrogant economists, Keynesians and socialists from assuming they could understand such dynamics and either steer them in the right direction or assume control of them through overt statism. The end result would be disastrous, since it entailed tinkering blindly with what one didn't understand. Left to its own devices the market was self-correcting. The depressions and dynamic business cycles so decried by the left were indeed tragic, since on occasion people failed to respond to market signals effectively, or worse, they intervened to disrupt its operations. In these circumstances an economic downturn was a lamentable but necessary medicine to cleanse bad investments and weak firms from the market. The left didn't understand this and was determined to exercise state power to prevent this self-correcting process from running its court. In *The Road to Serfdom* Hayek famously prophesized this would also have more than just deleterious economic effects. As the negative material impacts of intervention became apparent, these arrogant planners would double down on the illusion that the problem was simply not planning well enough. When material deprivation generated agitation, they would seize more and more power, bringing about a kind of totalitarian society akin to Nazi Germany or the Soviet Union,

The paradoxical qualities of this reasoning are rather transparent. On the one hand the market is to be treated as a sublime object, beyond our full capacity to understand or control. On the other we can indeed know that the market is beneficent, and that even if no one can control the market we can nonetheless impact and damage it through interventionist policies. This echoes many other paradoxes which emerge in the conservative thinking that influenced many neoliberals; for instance, Edmund Burke's claim that tradition constituted a kind of embedded wisdom we cannot fully understand through reason but can nevertheless know is wisdom. At a more practical level one might ask how the neoliberals are certain that interventions, even if they produce unintended effects, will nonetheless be bad. It could well be that the unintended effects of economic intervention will be positive; for instance, policies to reduce poverty may inadvertently cut down on health costs. What backs up their anxieties is therefore less economic analysis and more a normative disposition; that we should err on the side of restraint rather than optimism and experimentalism because the failure to do so might be disastrous. Moreover there is more than a little bit of a quasi-religious dimension to this, since many of their writings suggest tinkering with the market is also irreverent. It displays a kind of Luciferean hubris to assume we could do better than the market which evolved to service our needs. It's in these moments especially that the sublimated dimensions of market ideology become most clear and humorous.

Civilization Must Be Defended

The central values of civilization are in danger. Over large stretches of the Earth's surface the essential conditions of human dignity and freedom have already disappeared. In others they are under constant menace from the development of current tendencies of policy. The position of the individual and the voluntary group are progressively undermined by extensions of arbitrary power. Even that most precious possession of Western Man, freedom of thought and expression, is threatened by the spread of creeds which, claiming the privilege of tolerance when in the position of a minority, seek only to establish a position of power in which they can suppress and obliterate all views but their own. The group holds that these developments have been fostered by the growth of a view of history which denies all absolute moral standards and by the growth of theories which question the desirability of the rule of law. It holds further that they have been fostered by a decline of belief in private property and the competitive market; for without the diffused power and initiative associated with these institutions it is difficult to imagine a society in which freedom may be effectively preserved.
Statement of Aims, Mont Pelerin Society

The neoliberals recognized that capitalism could only be truly safe from the democratic nation-state and other political pressures through the creation of an international system of regulations and institutions. These would ultimately be backed up by American military power and the hegemony of the Washington consensus, creating a global economic order that would last for 40 years.

The first generation of neoliberal theorists were largely Europeans, including many expats who fled to the United States in the face of Nazi aggression. Their early theorizing is sometimes characterized as the Austrian School; so named because many of the neoliberals – including Hayek, von Mises and Carl Menger – came of age in the cosmopolitan Austro-Hungarian Empire. As mentioned they were horrified by the spread of Nazism and Bolshevism on the continent, seeing them as little more than two sides of the same coin. As mentioned some of them, like von Mises, initially had some initial sympathy for the efforts of fascists to halt the spread of communism and protect private property through the auspices of a powerful state. Wilhelm Ropke had comparatively repellent views on the virtues of South African apartheid, even publishing a book defending it in 1964. But whatever popularity such views had soured when it became clear that fascism was headed for the moral abyss, and eventually the prevailing opinion was very similar to Hayek's pox on both their houses. Unfortunately for them, at the end of the Second World War there was little ideological or political appetite for their brand of free market dogmatics. This explained the rather shrill apocalyptics which marked early neoliberalism, also the melodramatic reference to the "central values of civilization" being in mortal danger.

Despite some post-war pessimism, they wouldn't have to wait long to find a receptive audience. By the 1950s a generation of economists and free market thinkers were emerging from American universities eager to respond to the dangerous collectivism and radicalism of the time. Most prominent among them was the infamous Chicago School; so named because of the militantly anti-Keynesian approach of the Economics Department at the University of Chicago through the 1950s and 60s. Luminaries included Milton Friedman, Gary Becker and Thomas Sowell. Hayek himself was in frequent contact with members of the Chicago School and was even a faculty member on the Committee of Social Thought during the 1950s. Like the earlier generations of neoliberals in the Mont Pelerin Society, Friedman et al saw the fundamental values of a free society as being threatened by the spread of "collectivist" ideas. In his 1962 bestseller *Capitalism and Freedom,* Friedman echoes these anxieties and gave them a nostalgic and patriotic twinge. He ruminated on how the country of his maturity looked different than that of his youth and lamented the transition from an allegedly "free" society to one where the government was expected to manage everybody. He argues that government should limit itself to enforcing the rule of law, and in particular property rights. Doing any more both prevented the market from allocating resources efficiently and was a fundamental threat to a free society. Intriguingly, Friedman even puts forward some innovative ideas, such as using negative income taxes to secure a guaranteed minimum income for all.

By the 1970s these neoliberal ideas had grown popular enough that the American government was willing to experiment with them. Ground zero was to be Chile in 1973. The Monroe Doctrine had been unofficial American policy for some time and had been given a vigorous shot in the arm by the Cuban revolution and the failure of the Bay of Pigs invasion. Many American analysts were deeply concerned at the possibility of a wave of socialist and leftist uprisings across Latin America which would destabilize their own back yard and likely create a crisis of legitimacy. When the Democratic Socialist Salvador Allende was elected President of Chile in 1970, it sent waves of anxiety through the American government, which promptly organized a coup to get rid of him. They put General Augusto Pinochet in power, who promptly initiated a wave of terror to crack down on his domestic enemies. This included the widespread use of torture, with over 30,000 victims.

Pinochet introduced the world's first comprehensive policy of neoliberalization. He declared that he wanted Chile to be a nation of "proprietors" and not "proletarians." This included de-nationalizing the mining industry, privatizing health and education services, cutting family allowances, and encouraging borrowing from financial conglomerates to fund investment and competition. Property which had been expropriated during the Allende regime was returned. It was a textbook example of neoliberal reforms: supply side economics, the state enforcing property rights and the rule of law with a heavy hand, and the liquidation of public assets. The result was initially encouraging to the Chicago School economists. Chile experienced high levels of GDP growth and the return of foreign capital, though this was accompanied by skyrocketing inequality and very bad living conditions for the poorest Chileans. Milton Friedman prematurely spoke about the "miracle of Chile." Things got worse in the 1980s when the Latin American debt crisis hit Chile hard, and Pinochet lost a great deal of his support during a difficult recession. In 1988 the country transitioned back to being a partial democracy, though Pinochet would retain several prestigious offices and his allies remained in positions of power and influence. Despite these safeguards, his sins nearly caught up with him. In the late 1990s, Pinochet was abroad seeking medical treatment when he was extradited to the United Kingdom and charged with various crimes before the British House of Lords. He likely would have faced justice had it not been for the intervention of Margaret Thatcher and George W. Bush on his behalf; proof positive that the largest barrier to building an international justice system is often powerful Western leaders and states.

Not ones to be deterred, neoliberals experienced a

tremendous shot in the arm during the 1980s with the elections of Ronald Reagan and Margaret Thatcher. Both of them embodied the new ethos of stripping away the welfare state while encouraging competition, a firm law and order policy and muscular foreign policies. They also dramatically reoriented the approach in international financial and aid organizations toward investment. The World Bank and International Monetary Fund tied the reception of loans and development monies to the implementation of neoliberal reforms in recipient countries. These were often carried out under the innocuous heading of "structural adjustment programs." Most of them were carried out in African and Latin American countries, and included the typical recipe of entrenching property rights, opening to foreign investment, privatizing state assets wherever possible, and of course gutting welfarist programs. The stated justification was the need to make these countries more competitive in an increasingly globalized world, where capital could move its assets and industries without inhibition. Simultaneously the availability of vast new reserves of labor in the developing world enabled neoliberal politicians to pressure unions and labor organizations into making concessions, or even dissolving them outright. The result was greater worldwide economic integration, and the period saw the emergence of NATO, the European Union and the World Trade Organization as major international regulators aimed at facilitating the flow of capital and goods across the globe. The latter was especially significant in being one of the first major organizations whose sole job was to regulate and enforce global trade policy, and nothing else.

The impact of these policies was often dramatic. After initiating a series of neoliberal reforms in the 80s and 90s, Brazil had one of the highest rates of inequality in the world, with a GINI coefficient of 0.6 – higher than the United States at the same time. Despite this about 12-15 percent of the population still lived in endemic poverty; often made worse by the precarity of the new, short-term jobs introduced by reforms. These inequalities often intersected with others along racial and gender lines. The result was widespread anger, and the election of Lula and the Workers Party in 2003. A similar story can be told about Greece in the lead up to the 2015 financial crisis. Integration into the global economy allowed many rich Greeks to avoid paying taxes. The exact amount is impossible to know but estimates ran from between 10-30 billion USD a year – a substantial part of Greece's GDP. Nevertheless, the state borrowed heavily to continue providing services and to try and make the country competitive in a European context. All this came to a head in 2015 when Syriza, a left-wing party, attempted to negotiate with European financiers and the IMF to curb Greek debt and stabilize the economy. Syriza was forced to implement major austerity measures, despite a popular referendum rejecting them, under threat of not receiving enough assets to bail out the economy.

Conclusion: All That Is Solid Melts into Air

Starting in the early seventies you do have this sense amongst the capitalist class that there's a lot of momentum on the other side of the equation...from anti-colonialist liberation movements across Africa, Asia, Latin America which have nationalist aspirations and almost always some type of Marxist discourse in socialist politics and that implicates what already was...Then also in Europe, increasingly radical labor demands and this is of course connected with various political tendencies. But in the right-wing mind everything under the umbrella – from civil rights, women's rights, the student, to ecological justice, and accelerated labor demands [are currents] leading up to neoliberalism.
Michael Brooks, Neoliberalism: A Primer.

These examples demonstrate both the corrosive effect of

neoliberalization, and also its distinctive features compared to earlier forms of capitalism. Neoliberals like Friedman and Hayek often spoke a great deal about shrinking the state, or the dangers of the "big state." Indeed sometimes there could be a distinctly libertarian air to their rhetoric, which has sometimes led commentators to conflate the two together. But in fact neoliberals actually held elements of the state in high regard; as Hayek observed time and again, what he wanted was freedom through the law, not freedom from state coercion. He recognized that a sufficiently strong state would be necessary to both entrench property rights, maintain order, and in the worst case scenario eliminate various forms of dissent ala Pinochet and even South Africa. The neoliberals also recognized how contingent a hold on state power could genuinely be; the experience of the mid-century had shown how socialist and social democratic movements could be genuinely popular and win power even in large capitalist countries like the United Kingdom and West Germany. So further safeguards for capital needed to be constructed at the international level. To this day when most leftists are critical of globalization and liberal cosmopolitanism, it is this neoliberal project they are implicitly or explicitly rejecting: the ideal of a harmonious globe of free moving capital and sovereign states, each responsible for encasing the dynamic markets from domestic pressures and backed up by international legal institutions and American military power.

The result was a world remade more dramatically than ever in the image of capital, and the breakdown of many of the remaining traditionalist and localist barriers to its colonization. The kind of post-modern societies which emerged have been discussed at length in some of my other books, such as *What is Post-Modern Conservatism?* Here I'd like to discuss a different dimension to neoliberal internationalism, which is its ideological supplement: neoconservatism. The link between neoliberalism and neoconservatism has often been undertheorized, with many assuming neoconservatism's distinctly anti-internationalist outlook would be kryptonite to many neoliberals. As we'll see, this was hardly the case, and in many respects neoconservatism enabled neoliberalism to function by empowering American military and political elites to direct their yearning for historical significance beyond the possibilities offered by market society into projects of more directly remaking the world.

Chapter Three

Neoconservatism, Post-Modern Conservatism and Global Capitalism

A Society Focused on the Next Refrigerator

Neoconservatism had its intellectual roots in disaffected leftists and liberals who were troubled by the American public's response to the Vietnam war and the general decadence of the era. Many of them were influenced by the neo-classicist philosophy of Leo Strauss, a German-Jewish émigré of the Nazi regime who developed a novel conservative critique of modernity. For Strauss, modern liberal societies were oriented by a permissive ethic that saw freedom as the pure pursuit of one's desire. This was reflected in the conception of rights put forward by liberals, which in a Millsian vein tended to emphasize an individual's entitlement to do whatever they wished so long as they didn't harm or interfere with the freedom of others. The best kind of political order was consequently one which granted and guaranteed the broadest array of liberal rights. For Strauss, liberalism was misguided in its assumption that freedom simply meant doing whatever one wanted. Going back to Plato, he appealed to more ancient and venerable conceptions of freedom which conceived it as aligning the soul with higher forms of excellence.

This has an inevitably hierarchical quality to it, both in Plato and Straussianism, since this conception of freedom was paradoxically demanding rather than permissive. It sometimes necessitated the renunciation of banal and decadent desires to devote one's self intellectually to contemplating and developing the qualities required to be excellent. This would in the end permit them to enjoy a higher kind of freedom than that offered by mere possessive liberalism. Many people would lack either the intelligence or dedication to do so, and those that did were naturally better equipped to lead the mere masses, who often dedicated themselves to the pursuit of the venal and immediate. For Straussians the goal of a classical education was to produce just such leaders through an emphasis on the classical texts and their canonical progeny. In 1987 Allan Bloom, one of the most emblematic Straussians, published his book *The Closing of the American Mind*. Very much of a piece with this thinking it was one of the major conservative shots in the burgeoning culture war, arguing that elite universities increasingly failed to teach their students the classics and instead imparted a kind of cheesy, hip relativism. In a rather amusing passage, Bloom waxes poetic about the evil gyrating hips of Mick Jagger of the Rolling Stones, seeing him as an embodiment of everything that was wrong with the modern word.

The neoconservatives diagnosed both the ultra-permissiveness of the Sixties and the New Left, along with the widespread unwillingness of American youth to go fight and die in Vietnam, on these lines. They saw it as reflecting the declining emphasis on virtue and civic mindedness in American culture, and its replacement with a do as you feel attitude that aspired to nothing higher than self-gratification and a kind of New Age self-realization. But, like Strauss, they were never quite willing to fully give up on liberalism, and (unlike Strauss' more critical approach to the market) they were certainly not opposed to capitalism. After all, the most venerable mores in American society were undeniably liberal and ruthlessly capitalistic. Moreover, going back to the revolution the most patriotic Americans had always been convinced that their country had a unique destiny; to serve as the "shining city on the hill" as the TV president Ronald Reagan put it, or the "indispensable" nation as put by Sidney Blumenthal and James Chace. The neoconservative project became one to synthesize the disciplined pursuit of excellence put forward by classicists like Strauss with a muscular liberal capitalism that would be committed to more than just sex, drugs and rock and roll.

The solution became to focus on an external threat to the United States which could serve to mobilize people's passions and commit themselves to the grand project of preserving and advancing the American way across the globe; securing worldwide hegemony in less politically correct words. For a long time neoconservative didn't have to look very far. They applauded the resumption of Cold War animosity during the Reagan years, backing the most militant and assertive efforts to bring down the evil empire of the Soviets. Jeane Kirkpatrick's 1979 essay "Dictatorships and Double Standards," which criticized the Carter policy of détente with the Soviets and other left-wing autocracies, was emblematic. Many of them celebrated rapturously in 1989 when it became clear that the Soviet bloc was crumbling and would – at least at first – be replaced by a new assembly of representative democracies with mixed or mostly capitalist economies. But this quickly raised the question of what new enemy could serve as a sufficiently dangerous foil to inspire Americans and their allies to great projects and commitments. In his most neoconservative phase, a young Francis Fukuyama wrote "The End of History?" and argued that individuals with a strong yearning for thymotic recognition – world historical significance – may well be inspired to restart history just to get the aplomb they feel they deserve. The *Project for the New American Century* put it even more vividly in a 2000 report, warning that if Americans got complacent and allowed themselves to enjoy the spoils of peace and contentment, the result would be a new series of enemies rising.

In other words, until another great power challenger emerges, the United States can enjoy a respite from the demands of international leadership. Like a boxer between championship bouts, America can afford to relax and live the good life, certain that there would be enough time to shape up for the next big challenge. Thus the United States could afford to reduce its military forces, close bases overseas, halt major weapons programs and reap the financial benefits of the "peace dividend." But as we have seen over the past decade, there has been no shortage of powers around the world who have taken the collapse of the Soviet empire as an opportunity to expand their own influence and challenge the American-led security order.

This well articulates the fundamental anxiety of neoconservatism, which is that neoliberalism and markets are all well and good. But if all Americans and their allies come to fixate on is how to build and consume better refrigerators and Big Macs, their cultures will become excessively materialistic and decadent. This is the inevitable start of decadence and then decay. The United States needs to retain its martial edge and discipline, which will include maintaining a vast military presence, if it is to stave off the decline that has befallen empires past. Much of this was of course affirmed by a variety of think tanks well-funded by the weapons and oil industry.

Through the 1990s a variety of different, potential tasks and enemies were put forward by neoconservatives. In 1996 the political scientist Samuel Huntington published *Clash of Civilizations* in response to Fukuyama's essay. It hypothesized that in place of the grand, tripartite ideological struggles of the twentieth century – fascism vs communism vs liberal capitalism – the twenty-first century would be defined by the titular clash of civilizations. The book was widely criticized for playing rather fast and loose with what was entailed by these civilizations. Often it seemed to rely on rather broad cliches which bordered on prejudices; when ruminating on why Australia was unlikely to join "Eastern civilization," Huntington opined that it was unlikely that a boisterous people like the Australians would feel a lot of affinity for stoic Asians inspired by Buddhist philosophy. There are also many questions you have to ask about why Latin America isn't immediately associated with the "Western" world. They're among the most Christian countries in the world, all former European colonies, and predominately speak Spanish and Portuguese. It's hard to not simply assume Huntington excludes them for either not being rich enough or for more obviously racialized reasons. But the idea was sufficiently popular to remain relevant well into the twenty-first century when post-modern conservative Trumpists adopted the "clash" rhetoric to justify their xenophobic policies. Some neoconservatives were more conventional and simply swapped China for the Soviet Union as the new great power with which the United States had to compete. This failed to gain a great deal of traction during the 1990s when China largely pursued a policy of foreign policy isolationism while simultaneously shifting its economy toward further neoliberalization. But it also received a big shot in the arm under the superficially anti-neocon President Donald Trump, who invoked a lot of Sinophobic rhetoric and engaged in a lengthy trade war with the middle kingdom.

The War on Terror I: Empire Lite

The aide said that guys like me were "in what we call the reality-based community," which he defined as people who "believe that solutions emerge from your judicious study of discernible reality."..."That's not the way the world really works anymore," he continued. "We're an empire now, and when we act, we create our own reality. And while you're studying that reality – judiciously, as you will – we'll act again, creating other new realities, which you can study too, and that's how things will sort out. We're history's actors...and you, all of you, will be left to just study what we do.
Quote widely attributed to Karl Rove

But, of course, the primary enemy selected and constructed was so called "radical Islamic terror." This had its roots in everything from the longstanding American alliance with Israel to resentment over the 1979 Iranian revolution, which saw the US puppet Shah replaced by a brutal Shia fundamentalist regime under the leadership of Ayatollah Khomeni. It got a substantial shot in the arm during the 1990s. George Bush Sr launched a successful and UN-backed war in the Gulf regime to drive former American ally Saddam Hussein from oil-rich Kuwait. This was heavily theorized at the time, with neoconservatives seeing the Gulf War as expelling the ghost of Vietnam and showcasing the potential of US military power to effectively police the globe. On the other end of the spectrum the post-Marxist theorist Jean Baudrillard infamously proclaimed that the Gulf War "did not take place." It was a manufactured conflict more valuable to the Americans for the hyperreal images it produced on round-the-clock cable news, showcasing the power of new military technologies and glorifying in the capacity of the military to destroy the Iraqi army at minimal cost to themselves. The 25,000-50,000 Iraqis who died for the sake of such sensationalism were scarcely a presence, since displaying them would have been an all-too-visible return of the real into the phantasma of libidinal enjoyment. On the other end a series of terrorist attacks, most notably the 1993 bombing of the World Trade Center and the bombing of the USS Cole, generated a manic sense of fear and anxiety; a realization that for all its power, the empire remained vulnerable to attack by dedicated militant groups with a fraction of the resources and influence.

This back-and-forth in the approach to "radical Islamic terror" – on the one hand glorifying in one's omnipotence relative to it, and on the other presenting it as an existential threat to the American way – may well appear to be contradictory. But, in fact, the structure of ideology often functions in just such a manner, as a means of papering over more fundamental material contradictions. The presentation of "radical Islamic terror" as both the purview of a few primitive barbarians and a danger to the world's greatest military was necessary to simultaneously vindicate a struggle against real danger while never ceding any cultural or religious ground to the radicals, or at its highest pitch Islam itself. It was necessary for Islamic terrorists to be simultaneously dangerous and pitiful at the same time. If they weren't dangerous then there would be no reason to struggle. If they weren't pitiful, it would suggest they possessed genuine human qualities and may legitimately have had grievances against the exercise of American power which explained their actions. This isn't to justify terror, of course – which can never be justified. But it explains how the simultaneous elevation and denigration of an ideological opponent serves to both dehumanize them and dissociate from the real material facts of geopolitics which give rise to violence. In this case the long history of American interventionism, support for authoritarianism, and corruption in the Middle East, following on the heels of a long history of European imperialism and colonialism in the region that dates back to the 1850s when the British annexed Pakistan to the Raj.

All these tendencies would become radicalized during the course of the War on Terror. September 11, 2001 was a formative moment in my life, being perhaps the first bit of news I genuinely remember fixating on. Even in Canada our school was immediately evacuated and downtown Ottawa became a ghost town. The tragedy of such a senselessly violent event, butchery on a mass scale, necessitated some response. Unfortunately the response we got was entirely the wrong one, and both the United States and especially the Middle East would suffer from the incompetence of what followed.

The neoconservative response to 9/11 was one of the most callow instances of political opportunism in recent memory. Many of them believed that their time had come, since there was finally both a sympathetic president in the White House and a public willingness to deploy American military power for the kind of grandiose projects they yearned for. Much of the delusion that American-style capitalism and representative democracy could be easily exported at the barrel of a gun was inspired by the singular experience of the post-Cold War transition in Eastern Europe. It was assumed that, just as many of those countries readily transitioned to representative democracies with capitalist markets with the fall of the Soviet Empire, so too would the people of Afghanistan and Iraq readily line up for committee meetings, the Simpsons and McDonald's if just given the opportunity. This almost child-like naivete was accompanied by a distinctly post-modern variation of Augustine's libido domanandi. Where St Augustine believed the yearning for power reflected a longing to rule God's creation, neoconservatives went a step further in being convinced that even the materiality and historicity of reality was no inherent limitation on the exercise of imperial power. This epistemic conception of the world and communities as plastic mediums through which imperial power works had been well primed by the hyperreal exercise of American power during the 1990s, but few things could have prepared us for the sheer impotent bigness of the Bush Jr administration.

One of the most distinctly vacuous neologisms invented to describe this new reality was Michael Ignatieff's "empire lite" in his 2003 book *Empire Lite: Nation Building in Bosnia, Kosovo and Afghanistan.* Ignatieff would later go on to have a remarkably disastrous career in Canadian politics, confirming his qualities as a political analyst. But before then he sought to defend the idea of using American military power to reconstruct nation-states along liberal-capitalist lines, including defending the use of torture and "enhanced interrogation" as "lesser evils" in the fight against terrorism. What made Ignatieff's analysis especially noxious was the way it effectively tried to sanitize the exercise of power and violence in the pursuit of global hegemony; enough to make one yearn for the good old-fashioned, honest brutality of the Athenian delegation to Melos when they claimed, "we will not trouble you with specious pretense." The premise of "empire lite" was that we should welcome a PC iteration of imperial hegemony; largely painless, and free from many (though by no means all) the negative associations conjured by imperium past. Empire lite would be humanitarian, promote democracy and respect for human rights across the globe, and generally benevolent in its intent. Naturally Ignatieff had little to say about the political economy of such a neoconservative hegemony, fascinated exclusively by the specter of its liberal overtones. The remarkably self-serving ways American industry and its allies integrated themselves into the exploitation of post-war Iraq, the indifferent offshoring of the War in Afghanistan to mercenaries and local militias little supported by the population, and the resilience of clannish and kleptocratic networks of power and affluence in the face of marketization were all swept aside in this simulacrum of international realism.

It's a testament to the poverty of this view that even its moderate concessions to a more brutal realism about power ended up being exploded over the course of a few years. "Empire" lite in practice wound up acting very like empires of yore; distinct only in the level of incompetence and needless violence on display. As is well known neither the war in Iraq nor Afghanistan ended on a high note. Despite hundreds of thousands of civilian and military dead, trillions spent on reconstructive efforts, and various surges and renewed efforts, by 2021 Iraq was just at the tail end of being dragged through a major regional civil war that erupted in Syria and quickly spread like wildfire when ISIS momentary gained ascendency. In a supreme irony it became increasingly clear that the Taliban would like to be restored to some semblance of power in

Afghanistan. More relevantly, both the United States and the kind of neoconservative unilateralism it espoused through the 1990s and 2000s saw its international reputation badly savaged. Domestically this would have truly dramatic effects; first the election of a more pacific Democrat in Barak Obama and more spectacularly with the election of the post-modern conservative Donald Trump into office in 2016. But before all this we need to look at how the United States and its allies caused significant damage to the Kantian cosmopolitan project that had been a hallmark of the post-war consensus.

The War on Terror II: The Attack on Cosmopolitan Institutions

The neoliberal assault on welfarism and its efforts to use international law to make the world safe for capital ensured that the most ambitious visions of cosmopolitanism popular during the mid-century would never come to fruition. But in the 1990s a more moderate but still grand ideal was resurrected: the Kantian cosmopolitan project of limiting the power of sovereign states to abuse the liberal rights of their citizens, and even to make certain kinds of state action criminally liable. We saw an example of this earlier on with the attempted and failed prosecution of Augusto Pinochet, who got away with literal murder due to having the right connections. But more successful efforts were launched in the former Yugoslavia after a long and brutal nationalist civil war broke out, marred by mass war crimes and genocide. After the war many members of Serbia's military elite, including former President Slobodan Milosevic, were put on trial at the International Criminal Tribunal for the Former Yugoslavia. This pioneering effort was followed by the International Criminal Tribunal for Rwanda and the Extraordinary Chambers in the Courts of Cambodia prosecuting the Khmer Rouge. Finally, in 1998, the *Rome Statute* established the International Criminal Court (or ICC as it's called). For this brief period, it genuinely looked like an international criminal justice system enforcing human rights – problematically backed by American military power – was emerging.

The notion of an international criminal justice system was never – and will never be – uncontroversial. With the exception of the Cambodian court, there were extensive criticisms of virtually every one of the examples listed. The Yugoslav tribunal was criticized for focusing excessively on crimes committed by the Serbs rather than their opponents, including NATO officials who launched aggressive campaigns with the sanction of the United Nations. The Rwanda tribunal was often castigated as too little, too late by critics who took issue with how Western states simply ignored the build-up to the genocide. And when they did pay attention to it, it was often depicted through a racialist lens and indicatory of African violence, with few efforts made to situate the roots of the genocide in the long history of European colonization in Rwanda. The International Criminal Court, which remains the crowning institution of the global criminal justice system, has similarly been long critiqued for focusing all its resources on prosecuting sub-Saharan Africans, while war crimes committed by the great powers invariably get a pass.

Saying that, it remains rather surprising how broad the support for creating an international justice system was during its heyday. Major leftist philosophers like Noam Chomsky and Jurgen Habermas signified their qualified support for the idea of restricting state power through legal instruments of worldwide legitimacy. While the world's major authoritarian regimes naturally didn't back it, most of Latin America and sub-Saharan Africa became signatories to the Rome Statute for a complex array of moral and geopolitical considerations. And it must be said that the idea that no one, even heads of state, is above the law has a kind of liberal (in the best sense) appeal to it. If the twentieth century proved anything, it is that powerful states can be a bigger threat to individual rights and safety than Hobbes' natural warre of all against all ever could be. However fickle, providing some mechanisms of accountability – not to mention granting the often victims of violence a sense that justice will be done – was surely an admirable enterprise on principle. And it did have some major successes; from bringing a former head of state like Milosevic to trial, providing a forum for the stories of victims to be aired, and even prompting important theoretical ruminations, like Catherine MacKinnon's on the connections between state violence and patriarchal culture.

The neoconservatives were among the most committed opponents of the mere idea of an international justice system and remain so to this day. Perhaps the most articulate and passionate opponent remains John Bolton, who was not at all shy about expressing his one-sided and self-serving rationales for opposing it. Here is a 2018 speech he gave on the ICC to the conservative Federalist Society, while still momentarily serving as a national security advisor in the Trump administration:

After years of effort by self-styled "global governance" advocates, the ICC, a supranational tribunal that could supersede national sovereignties and directly prosecute individuals for alleged war crimes, was agreed to in 1998. For ICC proponents, this supranational, independent institution has always been critical to their efforts to overcome the perceived failures of nation-states, even those with strong constitutions, representative government, and the rule of law. In theory, the ICC holds perpetrators of the most egregious atrocities accountable for their crimes, provides justice to the victims, and deters future abuses. In practice, however, the court has been ineffective, unaccountable, and indeed, outright dangerous. Moreover, the largely unspoken, but always central, aim of its most vigorous supporters was to constrain the United States. The objective was not limited to targeting individual US service members, but rather America's senior political leadership, and its relentless determination to keep our country secure.

In effect then, the problem with both the court and the notion of an international criminal justice system more generally is the challenge it poses to the legitimacy of American global hegemony. It exposed the one-sidedness of the United States and its allies' commitment to democracy and the rule of law, which they were happy to appeal to when applying it elsewhere but deeply self-conscious of when the same expectations were imposed on them. And the response of American neoconservatives was more than mere expressions of cultural and nationalist animosity. Both the Bush and Trump administrations launched substantial assaults on the international legal order the United States had, ironically, done much to create. Few were as mercifully transparent about their jingoism as John Bolton, and the typical rhetorical strategy was to appeal to Westphalian notions of national and state sovereignty in contrast to the globalist ambitions of technocratic and unrooted cosmopolitan elites.

The Bush administration's weightiest blow against international cosmopolitanism was indirect. The 2001 invasion of Afghanistan was not explicitly legitimated by the United Nations, as 1991's Gulf War had been. But the UN and other cosmopolitan institutions also didn't object to the invasion, for a variety of moral and geopolitical reasons. There was a substantial amount of sympathy for the United States in the aftermath of the 9/11 attacks, and a more chilling appreciation that some kind of reprisal against American enemies was inevitable. As far as it went, the ruling Taliban, who were screening Al-Qaeda, seemed as innocuous a target as anywhere else.

Things were very different with the war in Iraq. It quickly became clear that, despite the lies of the Bush administration, Saddam Hussein and the Baathist regime had no ties to the fundamentalist groups that had planned and enacted the 9/11 terror attacks. When that didn't stick, the argument became that Hussein possessed weapons of mass destruction. But despite a lengthy investigation headed by Hans Blix, the United Nations investigators found little or no evidence that Hussein had or was producing weapons of mass destruction. Fortunately for Bush and the other criminals he surrounded himself with, reality proved a surprisingly light burden for global hegemons in the heated days of the early 2000s. In 2003 the United States brushed aside repeated warnings from the United Nations and worldwide protests involving millions of people, and invaded Iraq. The end result is by now extremely well known. The initial American invasion and counterinsurgency took the lives of hundreds of thousands of Iraqis, and thousands of American soldiers to boot. Just as consequential was the tremendous instability that was unleashed, which became a vital ingredient in the noxious stew leading to the rise of ISIL in the 2010s, which brought death to hundreds of thousands more in the region. As of writing this the country has just begun to tentatively recover, though insurrection persists in the north.

One might have thought that such a flagrant and damaging example of unilateralism, backed by its typically American mixture of blind idealism, naked self-interest, and indifference to cultural distinctiveness and regional history, would have been a catalyzing moment for cosmopolitans. After all, it was international institutions that sounded the warning against the war and made the most concerted effort to put the breaks on the US's imperial ambitions. But the damage had already been done. The United States had always been a tepid supporter of international institutions, seeing them as a means to advance its own interests primarily, or else falling victim to the conceit that its own approach to rights and politics was so self-evidently true any robust cosmopolitanism would inexorably align with its own values. But with the War on Terror, it firmly withdrew support, letting the fragile architecture put in place through the late twentieth century bear the burden of protesting the flagrant human rights abuses and war crimes committed by countries like Russia, China and Saudi Arabia. This isn't to say there haven't been serious efforts to keep the Kantian project of constraining state sovereignty and violence alive. The major international tribunals set up during the 1990s have continued their work. The International Criminal Court has remained active, prosecuting dozens of the world's worst people. In 2021 it even took the unprecedented step of deciding the court had the legal authority to investigate allegations that Israeli officials and servicemen had committed war crimes in the area controlled by the Palestinian authority. This was a bold move for the court to take; and one suspects at least partly inspired by the aforementioned criticism that it had so far directed too much energy on exclusively prosecuting crimes committed in Africa. The decision to investigate Israel was certainly a step in the right direction.

But there is no doubt that the cosmopolitan project has lumbered rather than sprinted since the early 2000s. The heady ambitions of the 1990s, when it seemed genuinely possible to construct an international legal system that would apply to the strong as well as the weak, have long since given in to a far more pragmatic and even tragic sensibility on the part of commentators and activists, leading some to ruminate on the wisdom of Thucydides' rumination that in global affairs the strong do as they will while the weak suffer as they must. Rectifying this fact will be one of the main tasks a cosmopolitan socialism will have to set for itself.

Neoconservatism as the Ideological Supplement to Neoliberalism

Neoconservatism and neoliberalism may, on the surface, appear to have relatively little in common beyond being distinct ideologies supported by many on the political right. Where neoliberalism was an ultimately far more influential logic of global economic governance and discipline, neoconservatism was very much an account of international relations and the kind of hegemonic political order that the United States should aspire to create. Where neoliberals stressed the power of the market to pacify the world through raising standards of living and integrating different nations together, neoconservatives were deeply concerned such a thoroughly marketized society would lead to decadence and a long-term decline in martial prowess. Neoliberalism was supposed to bring about the end of history, while neoconservatives flocked to write books on how history would inexorably continue.

Like any other seeming contradiction, this needs to be resolved dialectically through recognizing the ideologically co-determining dimensions of neoconservatism and neoliberalism. Neoconservatism is the ideological supplement to neoliberalism which enables the latter to stabilize itself through exporting its social contradictions abroad. This should be understood at three levels. The simplest is the classic Marxist sense in which the economic limitations of neoliberal capitalism could only ever be overcome through moving them around, creating new markets and sources of industry by force if necessary. Certainly the nation building exercises of neoconservatism, whether in Eastern Europe or more controversially the Middle East, had as a consequence the collapse of an alternative economic philosophy to capitalism. It opened the space for American and European advisors to play a key rule in adopting shock-capitalism principles in long-term command or kleptocratic economies. In the more galling example of Iraq and Afghanistan, this took on an even more blatant form as major industries came under the control of American capitalists. In this way neoconservatism enabled neoliberals to export their economic philosophy through force where required, often under the auspices of spreading "freedom." The second level was through absorbing surplus resources and labor into military efforts, rather than either directing them to the resolution of social problems and inequities or allowing them to fester into social discontent. In this neoconservatives and neoliberals overplayed their hand, as the sheer illegitimacy of the Iraq war produced mass protests and anger of the sort not seen since Vietnam. And far from being cheap and quick, the War on Terror drained trillions of dollars and has yet to end.

But there is a far more important sense in which neoliberalism and neoconservatism are ideological supplements; indeed were even conceived as such by supporters of both like Jonah Goldberg of the *National Review* and the *Project for the New American Century*. This was the need to stabilize neoliberalism through the projection of an "other" who would shore up support through the spread of terror, while simultaneously serving as an outlet for the thymotic energies of Western populations who could potentially grow bored and decadent with mere consumerism. This sentiment was well articulated, in a Nietzschean vein, by Francis Fukuyama in his initial essay "The End of History?" Far from exulting in the moment, he worries about the museum-like form our culture would take at the end of history; not coincidentally a theme later taken up by Mark Fisher in *Capitalist Realism*. As Fukuyama put it:

The end of history will be a very sad time. The struggle for recognition, the willingness to risk one's life for a purely abstract goal, the worldwide ideological struggle that called forth daring, courage, imagination, and idealism, will be replaced by economic calculation, the endless solving of technical problems, environmental concerns, and the satisfaction of sophisticated consumer demands. In the post-historical period there will be neither art nor philosophy, just the perpetual caretaking of the museum of human history. I can feel in myself, and see in others around me, a powerful nostalgia for the time when history existed. Such nostalgia, in fact, will continue to fuel competition and conflict even in the post-historical world for some time to come.

We might add not fears about the boredom that comes from a lack of struggle, but the potential discontent that lack of a real enemy may engender, for instance, around growing inequality and power inequities. As neoliberalism took over politics and assumed control of the nation-state and the international arena, the managed quality of superficially democratic institutions became ever more apparent.

What makes this neoconservative account interesting is it is really an acknowledgment of the nihilistic qualities of market society, so well diagnosed and critiqued by figures from Marx through to Adorno and Horkheimer. For all their apparent buoyancy about markets, including in their neoliberal form, neoconservatives recognized that the kind of crude egoistic materialism and anti-politics engendered by the belief in market rationalization and pacification had the potential to generate a sense of meaninglessness and disposability. Indeed at its apex it could precisely foster the kinds of depression so well discussed by Fisher and Fredric Jameson; the belief that nothing anyone does can ultimately matter, that the only horizons for the pursuit of human excellence are accumulation, capitalization and consumption, and that my ethical duty to society is to accept my subjectivity molded by the social imperatives of neoliberal governance. Any objection to this would be dismissed by the pieties of market ideology as irrational or impossible to satiate, and so potentially dangerous.

But rather than mobilize these convictions as a critique of neoliberal market society, the answer of neoconservatives was predictably to fetishize the values of market society. By transforming them into an ahistorical idol, neoconservatives then appealed to the values of market society as a way of justifying a kind of militaristic grand project which went beyond the purview of the market and superficially overcame its nihilistic materialism. Market society and its values became not just something to live within, but to fight and die on behalf of. In some respects we saw the culmination of Hobbes's competitive vision of life, internalized and chastened by the market domestically but expressed vividly in outright "warre" to extend it abroad. But in order to do that neoconservatives needed to project the specter of an enemy who, as mentioned, was simultaneously both an unworthy counterpart and a lethal threat. Typically, this was cast in racist terms as a foreign other, who lacked genuine universality for their own value system – and so who was irrevocably conceived of as primitive and wanting – but whose very primitiveness gave them an energy and anti-materialist immediacy that made them threatening. This also held up an uncomfortable mirror to our own society, which no longer had the will to fight for genuinely universal values, and consequently gave in to decadent permissiveness.

There could also be even more reactionary variations on this. Many of the neoconservatives were liberals or former leftists, and so tended to see the fetishization of market values as sufficient to mobilize support for the kind of grand projects paradoxically required to overcome the nihilism of market society. But for the more socially reactionary figures even this wasn't sufficient. It conceded too much to liberalism, which they conveniently extricated from the historical materiality of capital as an independent source of anomie. What was required to truly defend the values of market society on this conception was a kind of religious discipline and moralism. Early post-modern conservatives like Dinesh D'Souza even gave this a quasi-teleological gloss, arguing that these failures are what brought 9/11 down on the United States and the West more generally. As he put it in his book *The Enemy at Home:*

The cultural left in this country is responsible for causing 9/11...In faulting the cultural left, I am not making the absurd accusation that this group blew up the World Trade Center and the Pentagon. I am saying that the cultural left and its allies in Congress, the media, Hollywood, the nonprofit sector, and the universities are the primary cause of the volcano of anger toward America that is erupting from the Islamic world. The Muslims who carried out the 9/11 attacks were the product of this visceral rage – some of it based on legitimate concerns, some of it based on wrongful prejudice, but all of it fueled and encouraged by the cultural left. Thus without the cultural left, 9/11 would not have happened.

As I'll observe in the next section, this transition from the enemy abroad to the one at home demarcates the shift from neoconservatism and neoliberalism to post-modern conservatism. But for now it's important to recognize how these ideological supplements aspired to stabilize a fundamentally nihilistic society through providing a sense of fetishized and externalized transcendence. Neoconservatism sought in the battle against "Islamic fundamentalism" a sense of meaning which would allow them to live within the one-dimensional market society they'd done so much to bring about. The simultaneous repugnance and fascination with fundamentalism flowed from an anxiety that its seemingly resolute dedication to the religious life may in fact have been a purer answer than the kind of grab bag of market values and Christian moralism that neoconservatism wound up offering.

But in fact the kind of transcendence offered by neoconservative's grand projects of remaking the world was, like all forms of fetishism, always a kind of illusory idealism. It was stamped by the logic of the very society whose limitations it yearned to overcome. The materiality of history, which generated real differences in social relations, was ignored by neoconservatives who were convinced that the subjective application of power by the rulers of empire could remake the world rapidly and cheaply. This is because the world was conceived as nothing more than an infinitely plastic medium into which empire expressed its yearning for meaning through acts of militaristic creative destruction. In a Nietzschean vein we might say that the requirement to fetishize the values of market society in order to license such projects was arbitrary, since the ultimate point was always to enjoy the feeling of applying power over others in such efforts to remake plastic reality. Neoconservatism's overcoming of nihilism was nothing more than providing an outlet for the feelings of powerlessness ubiquitous in market society by allowing us to feel temporarily powerful merely because we can destroy, and destruction is a kind of proxy to genuine creation. But it ceased being Nietzschean in the sense that the neoconservatives were not at all the resentful weak of the world. Following Wendy Brown in her excellent book *In the Ruins of Neoliberalism*, we might say their resentment was that of the strong toward the limitations imposed on the exercise of imperial power. Neoconservatism allowed powerful American and Western figures to overcome their resentment at being stuck within the limitations of mere market society by allowing them to enjoy exercising their power against the wretched of the earth. In this respect post-modern conservatism constituted a continuation of neoconservatism, except directed inwardly first and foremost.

Post-Modern Conservatism and Nationalism

Americans, Poles, and the nations of Europe value individual freedom and sovereignty. We must work together to confront forces, whether they come from inside or out, from the South or the East, that threaten over time to undermine these values and to erase the bonds of culture, faith and tradition that make us who we are. If

left unchecked, these forces will undermine our courage, sap our spirit, and weaken our will to defend ourselves and our societies. But just as our adversaries and enemies of the past learned here in Poland, we know that these forces, too, are doomed to fail if we want them to fail. And we do, indeed, want them to fail.
Donald Trump, Speech in Poland July 6, 2017

The disastrous result of the neoconservative's global project, which most reasonable people rightly predicted could only end with death, impoverishment and shame, compelled a substantial rethink of the reactionary approach to global affairs. It became all too apparent that the ideal of remaking the world through the unilateral exercise of American power was an impossible and dangerous aspiration. On the other hand there was no stomach for resuscitating the all too liberal and tolerant dream of Kantian cosmopolitanism, in which Western societies would become but one more participant in a global republican order and which might impose moral and even legal constraints on the elite exercise of sovereign power. This was coupled with a growing wariness of neoliberalism, brought about by the uncertainty of the Great Recession and the naked exposure of how little power sovereign states now had in the face of pressure by domestic and international capital.

For a while there was some hope among liberals that the recession might trigger both a resuscitation of the cosmopolitan project and a resurgent but moderate neo-Keynesian kind of welfarism. Figures like Barak Obama and later Justin Trudeau embodied these ambitions. And in fact there were some interesting steps taken; most notably the introduction of Obamacare in the United States and Germany and France's decision to reinvest in post-secondary education to keep tuition costs very low. Moreover, under such conditions one would have thought that in such an environment the more radical solutions offered by the political left would have enjoyed real currency

14

with the broader population. And indeed some notable gains were made. Bernie Sanders and Jeremy Corbyn both beat the odds to become major players in American and British politics; at least temporarily in the former case. Lula da Silva's government saw a major boost in its prestige, as the Worker's Party became heralded for shepherding Brazil through the recession with minimal pain and a focus on the poor. Syriza came to power in Greece and momentarily looked like it might put the breaks on the harsh implementation of austerity in a country already wracked by inequality and the associated corruption. Bolivia under Evo Morales advanced a variety of programs to help the poor and did a great deal to integrate women and indigenous peoples into Bolivian society. Occupy Wall Street inspired sister protests in many countries, with its combination of radical utopianism and memorable slogans about the 99 percent. Even Karl Marx saw his reputation somewhat restored after the pits of the 1990s and early 2000s, and formerly stalwart capitalist outlets like *The Economist* and the *New York Times* published the occasional op-ed begrudgingly admitting he may have made a relevant point or two.

But generally speaking these successes were partial, often temporary and never mobilized into the kind of worldwide wave many of us were hoping for. There was little tangibly done to counteract the precarity and inequality generated by neoliberalism on a mass scale. Most of the stimulation packages conceived by post-Recession administrations were focused on bailing out the financial and corporate sectors, sometimes amounting to little more than overt bribes to keep them from slashing jobs (which many of them did anyways, as with the Oshawa car manufacturers in my own country). And they were often accompanied by intense austerity measures that doubled down on neoliberalization by insisting the answer to economic problems was to impose higher levels of fiscal discipline on poor and middle-income countries like Mexico and Greece, while compelling the more precarious populations of all countries to accept living with less.

In this environment the primary beneficiaries rather unexpectedly wound up being reactionary post-modern conservatives. The wave began in Hungary, Poland and India between 2010 and 2015, before growing into a tsunami with the election of Trump and Brexit in 2016. In 2018 the circus finally found its clown when Jair Bolsonaro was elected, ousting Lula's Workers Party on the back of a mass corruption scandal and growing discontent among affluent coastal Brazilians with their policies. Many of these figures emerged on the back of deepening discontent with the influence of global elites and their political representatives, who were portrayed as out of touch with the value systems of their national base and indifferent to the changing demographics and economic precarity brought about by neoliberal economics and overly permissive migration policies. This occasionally had a twinge of leftism about it, and occasionally post-liberal defenders of reaction like Patrick Deneen in *Why Liberalism Failed* would flirt with anti-capitalist rhetoric and policies. At its most theoretically ambitious this was presented as combining left-wing economics with militant social conservatism. Poland's Law and Justice government was usually held up as a model, with its Catholic approach to social policy coupled with generous welfarism; particularly the banner "500 Plus" program which made direct payments to families with young children. And indeed the potential popularity of such a combination was compelling enough that even erstwhile socialists like John B Judis in *The Socialist Awakening* called on leftists to embrace nationalism.

Post-modern conservatism's nationalist appeal arose in no small part precisely because of the tremendous instability generated by neoliberal capitalism. Neoliberalism's radical effort to break down global barriers had created a highly competitive and increasingly inegalitarian society, while also fundamentally changing the geographical and demographic makeup of society. Mass migration became the order of the day, while deepening urbanization and the shift to digital communications shifted the stakes in politics. The industrial revolution was giving way to the information economy, culturally prioritizing neoliberal elites who were able to access high levels of education at prestigious schools and institutions. This was accompanied by the proselytization of a meritocratic ethic which explained away the instability of these dynamics as a beneficial sign that capital and rewards were continuously being reallocated to the most productive and deserving. The flip side to this, of course, was that those left behind were cast as the unproductive and undeserving, and denied even the recourse of feudal ideology which held social divisions to be the product of a beneficent God. Instead they were held to be largely responsible for their failures; if anyone could make it with the right drive and intelligence, why couldn't they?

The emphasis on nationalism was given a distinctly agonistic twist by post-modern conservatives like Trump. In its heyday nationalism was often appealing to the political left as an identity that could summon mobilization against imperialism and the faux universalism of global capitalism. But it has also always had great appeal on the political right, for a variety of complex reasons. Conservative doctrine tends to oscillate widely between a fixation on the small and tradition on the one hand, and a source of transcendent meaning on the other. The relation between the two is subtle and varies depending on the kind of conservatism we are talking about. But broadly speaking the appeal of smallness and tradition to conservatism is the kind of ideological contentment it demonstrates with one's situation. As Roger Scruton put it in *The Meaning of Conservatism*, the emphasis on the small scale and empirically real is "a natural instinct in unthinking people – who, tolerant of the burdens that life lays on them, and unwilling to lodge blame where they seek no remedy, seek fulfillment in the world as it is – to accept and endorse through their actions the institutions and practices into which they are born." Such a disposition is of course well suited to accepting authority. By contrast the emphasis on the transcendent and gigantic is the flip side of the conservative disposition; an effort to sublimate power by transforming it into authority. Typically this is done through a process of naturalization, mythologization or both. The sublimation of power as authority is typically intended to remove it permanently from political contest, or at their most radical, even analysis. Edmund Burke's gothic characterization of society as an enduring contract between the dead, the living and those not yet born is representative. It also provides a sense of calcified meaning which comes from embedding one's self within sublimated power structures rather than contesting them, and even seeing their maintenance as the only bulwark against decadence and decline. In this respect power invites us to libidinally invest it with significance as a guarantor of both identity and ontological stability.

This was naturally extremely appealing for many under the conditions of post-modernity; offering a renewed sense of order and selfhood in a world increasingly bereft of them. The allure was even greater when it became clear that the nation-state was one of the few mechanisms available which still had the capacity to rein in the excesses of neoliberalization. One of the distinctive features of post-modern conservatism was an effort to capture the nation-state on behalf of a deserving group which was held as being left behind by globalization. But it did so without fundamentally challenging the inequities and power relations of capitalism. Post-modern conservatism's targets weren't inequality or capital, but the weak. Specifically post-modern conservatism attacked migrants, LGBTQ individuals, ethnic minorities and more through claiming they'd been given undeserved head starts through a combination of neoliberal internationalism and more conventional liberal cultural politics. In this respect it continued to reflect the meritocratic and competitive ethos of neoliberalization, but simply gave it a more ethnocentric and reactionary twist. Neoliberals and liberal cultural elites had opened the door to granting marginalized groups rights to compete in market society, even going so far as to break down the borders that posed limits on the mobility of capital and potential sources of cheap labor. Consequently the goal of the state was to eliminate such barriers while insulating capitalism from democratic pressure. Post-modern conservatives accepted the hierarchical logic of market society, but denied that such groups should be entitled to compete on an equal footing with the more deserving. The goal of its nationalism was therefore to restore the dignity and status of those groups post-modern conservatives felt were deserving through putting the undeserving back in their place using the power of the state. This power would of course be exercised by strong men like Trump or Victor Orban, who presented themselves as larger-than-life figures who resentful reactionaries could invest their faith in.

Conclusion: The Need for Cosmopolitan Socialism

Many people remain confused by post-modern conservatisms' contradictions; particularly its appeal to realism and folksy populism on the one hand and its spectacularly hyperreal approach to truth and facticity on the other. But the two are fundamentally related, insofar as crude and undynamic realism always transforms into a kind of vulgar idealism. Post-modern conservatives have a vision of how the world naturally "is" which they cling to with stubborn persistence. When inevitably things change, in no small part thanks to the transformative dynamics of the market, this generates resentment and the fantasia that only a sufficiently powerful source of national authority – like a strong man – can restore order. This source of authority is invested with a kind of transcendent and sublimated allure, as the one thing that can restore the ideal "natural" state of affairs. But, of course, since the underlying material dynamics remain unchallenged and indeed are reinforced by post-modern conservatism, it only serves to compound the problem. Its fantasia is never actually brought about, which only serves to intensify reactionary anxiety and resentment and leads to demands that more power be granted to the sublimated authority figure. The dangers of this became apparent during the COVID epidemic, when post-modern conservatives like Victor Orban and Donald Trump tried very hard to seize authoritarian power. The riots on January 6, 2021 in Washington DC, ending with the storming of Capitol Hill, showed just how close they came.

Such dangers demonstrate why cosmopolitan socialism is more vital than ever before. As the last two chapters have shown, for the past 4 decades the international arena has been dominated by neoconservatism, neoliberalism and now post-modern conservatism. The result has been dramatic inequality, pointless wars, and resurgent authoritarianism in countries many once thought were stalwarts of democracy. But cosmopolitan socialism can't just make the fall into the temptations of Kantian internationalism or the mere endorsement of a new kind of welfarism.. It needs to be far more ambitious in its vision and hard headed in its willingness to tackle power.

Chapter Four

What Would a Cosmopolitan Socialism Look Like?

The Lessons of Militant Particularism

A cosmopolitan socialism would be a socialism that accepted no arbitrary boundaries in its moral concern to achieve a life of flourishing for all. This would be distinct since, as discussed in Chapter One, most variants of socialism which have existed were either theoretically or practically committed to realizing the ideal at the nation-state level. In some respects this is eminently understandable. Despite relentless critiques of its violence, most socialists recognized that the kind of large-scale changes in political economy they aspired to would require a powerful instrument like the state to achieve. This was as true of the revolutionary as the reformist tradition. However, the negative consequence of this state-centrism was, in practice, that socialist movements never mounted a significant moral or geopolitical challenge to state sovereignty and its underlying dynamics. Indeed socialist regimes were all too often corrupted by the elixir of state power, and not a few transformed into authoritarian kleptocracies or outright totalitarian regimes. One of the virtues of a cosmopolitan socialism would be to wean socialism off of this temptation.

Associated with this must be a willingness to adopt a kind of moral universalism. This will undoubtedly be controversial. Since the 1960s, with the rise of what David Harvey calls militant particularism, universalism has been taboo on the left. Politically it is associated with the kind of imperialist logics most recently associated with neoliberalism and neoconservatism. Theoretically it is criticized for denying the ontological and moral significance of difference, and therefore justifying the imposition of power to efface distinct modes of being in the world. And these are undoubtedly real dangers that any kind of universalism risks falling into. The kind of anti-essentialist arguments about identity put forward by militant particularism, which denies that we have a teleological nature we should be beholden to in addition to rejecting the various ways we are interpellated as subjects by power, are extremely helpful in this regard. Conservative forms of essentialism have tried to insist either that identity remains fixed by nature, or set by conformity to social traditions and authorities, and consequently shouldn't be challenged. This of course plays a vital ideological role in maintaining support for the social hierarchies organized on the basis of fixed identities; whether one talks about gender and sexual roles, ethnic status and more. Militant particularism's challenge to these forms of essentialism, and its insistence that it more often than not reflects a kind of discourse of knowledge-power, have been vital in loosening up our theoretical imagination about the possibilities entailed by reconceiving identity. Conceived in this way one can understand why Michael Brooks would argue anti-essentialism must be an essential part of any cosmopolitan socialism.

But from a moral point of view militant particularism's strident anti-universalism is also a dead end which can very easily lead back to certain conservative conclusions. Theoretically anti-universalistic leftists often ignore a fundamental contradiction at the heart of their doctrine. They simultaneously claim that all (or almost all, since reactionaries don't get a pass) cultural perspectives are morally equal, while denying that any kind of universalistic moral outlook can arbitrate between them. But this is in fact a contradiction since to say almost all cultural perspectives are morally equal presupposes a second order capacity for evaluation. Indeed a very strong one since claiming that all cultural perspectives are morally equal is to make an extremely global judgment. And not one which any serious thinking militant-particularist would hold to with absolute conviction, for the reasons below.

Even more concerning than this philosophical contradiction is the fact that many of the theoretical justifications for militant particularism actually have a deep elective affinity to the arguments for conservatism. You don't need to tell Edmund Burke, Michael Oakeshott, Robert Bork or Thomas Sowell that human communities are held to very different value systems that are shaped by their distinct traditions and histories. In the hands of a conservative these points are used to justify the moral priority of our own group over others; after all, we will always feel more loyal to people like ourselves than the "other" who shares none of that history and identity. Conservatives will also point to the distinctiveness of cultural values to justify the retention of unnecessary and marginalizing hierarchies. After all, virtually every culture out there has developed robust arguments for the maintenance of patriarchy, sexual discrimination, religious and ethnic xenophobia. These could all be justified on the basis of preserving intact one's cultural way of life, and not giving in to faux universalistic arguments about the dignity or worth of all individuals. At its most robust, conservatism and militant particularism can even share a draconic anti-individualism, in the sense that the values of a shared identity can overrule a person's freedom. The "imagined community" of nationalism discussed in the last chapter is a good example. In this respect the shared identity is held to have a moral worth that outweighs that of the actually existent people that make it up. This is very much a kind of argument for transcendent difference that it has been the job of critical theory since Kant to reject.

Ironically one of the virtues of militant particularism has been its challenge to such cultural traditions where they pose a substantial barrier to inclusion. But it has never conceived of a theoretically satisfying justification for these practices, beyond a vague or even crypto-moral universalistic sense that a more inclusive and emancipated society is better than one dominated by traditionalist parochialism allied to capitalism.

Practically speaking militant-particularist anti-universalism has also run up against serious limits. In many countries it has motivated activist groups to make long-overdue demands for inclusion by historically marginalized groups. Some of these have been dramatically successful, as the spread of multicultural, feminist and LGBTQ acceptance has shown. But these demands for inclusion were often purchased at the cost of calling for structural change to material relations. Indeed what we call "woke capitalism" has demonstrated that neoliberalism is eminently compatible with demands for further inclusion; particularly where that provides an ideological justification for the market to further reify social differences as part of a continuous drive to create new commodified values. So we need a left which is able to retain militant particularism's paradoxically universalistic demand for inclusion while balancing that against a cosmopolitan effort to reform the global power dynamics of twenty-first century capital. As we will see below, this was something Michael Brooks was very good at.

Some will argue that this constitutes a regression to an earlier kind of leftist dogmatism which ignores the lessons of post-structuralism, Soviet totalitarianism and more besides. But there is no reason we cannot learn such lessons while remaining committed to a more inclusive, democratic and participatory universalism. We should be unafraid to argue that the demands of militant particularism are important. But not because a collective identity is morally important in itself. Rather collective identities are important because they matter to human beings, who do possess moral worth. And all human beings should be entitled to the freedom and material well-being necessary to lead a life of flourishing, which includes forming and indeed conserving meaningful shared identities over time. But these shared identities will always be internally and externally contested by those who reject the often hierarchical form they assume, or the exclusionary logic they can be predicated on. One of the virtues of socialism would be empowering individuals to engage in these kinds of agonistic contestations through democratic procedures, or even enabling them to withdraw from a shared identity and construct a new one for themselves.

Michael Brooks' Cosmopolitan Socialism I

Some leftists might resist the adoption of this kind of universal perspective – we, us, the human race – for at least two reasons. On one hand, Marxists might worry that it erases the distinction between different groups of humans with divergent economic interests. To my mind, though, this ignores the humanistic impulse that leads one to become a socialist in the first place. While it's true that struggling for a democratized economy means struggling against the segment of the population that benefits from the current undemocratic order, it's also true that, as Engels put it in The Anti-Dühring, *ending the division of society into contending social classes creates the possibility for a really human morality, universal in character.*
Michael Brooks, Against the Web

Michael Brooks' vision of cosmopolitan socialism is the right one for the contemporary left because it has internalized the lessons of militant particularism without surrendering a more expansive and global set of ambitions. As formulated by Brooks, cosmopolitan socialism was less a set of prescriptions or even an ethos. Instead it was rooted in a humanistic disposition in the best sense; as Terence would say, "nothing human" was foreign to it. Rather than give into the parochial temptation to privilege the accomplishments and needs of one's own people, Brooks was always sincerely interested in what other's thought, felt and achieved. And, of course, he was sensitive to the needless suffering we tolerate or forgive because many of us feel powerless to prevent it. Or worse still, we perpetuate it directly because it suits our interests. One of the few things Michael was unwilling to tolerate were tyrants, bigots and those who felt – as Ayn Rand did – that when they died the world came to an end. Michael passed away far too young, but he was well aware – as few of us are – of how much the lives of everyone else mattered as much as his own.

It was Michael's insistence that an injustice anywhere in the world was very much our business that gave this cosmopolitan and humanistic disposition a radical edge. In *Against the Web* he offered up a compelling critique of some of the most infamous reactionary and conservative intellectuals working today. The main butt of his argument is how the members of the intellectual dark web take an ahistorical approach when arguing for their political positions. Jordan Peterson excuses away vast disparities of wealth and power by arguing they flow from some kind of natural laws which are immutable and transhistorical. His justification is that even lobsters form hierarchies among themselves. Sam Harris argues that the history of American and European imperialism in the Middle East is irrelevant to considering how we should conceive of, and fight, twenty-first century terrorism. To him such a historical perspective gets in the way of being rational, by which Harris apparently means simultaneously calling for a radical war on Islam while castigating Muslims for holding to a violent and intolerant faith. In the *End of Faith* Harris borders on self-caricature when he waxes poetic about the dangers of a nuclear armed Islamic regime, before calling for a first strike that he admits will kill "tens of millions of innocents in a single day." Charles Murray argues that racial inequalities flow, not from generations of racist policies and slavery, but from genetic disparities in IQ we can do nothing to overcome. Worse still, he argues that any effort to try and improve the lot of the least well off will only take resources away from the more capable, and so should be avoided. Ben Shapiro asserts that the "West" is unique and special because of ideological commitment to both monotheism and Greek philosophy, while simply ignoring that Islam is also a monotheistic Abrahamic faith with many intellectual defenders who drew on the insights of Plato and Aristotle. But this hasn't kept him from relentlessly fear mongering about Islam.

By contrast Brooks always insisted we historicize political questions, looking at the complex material and geopolitical reasons why certain conflicts and disputes emerge. Peterson, Murray, Shapiro and Harris all in their own way try to suggest that the complex histories of marginalization, discrimination, imperialism and more don't matter very much when we ask political questions about economic and racial hierarchies, the geopolitics of Middle East, or in assessing our commonalities and differences with others. In this respect they even fall short of richer and more interesting conservative luminaries like Edmund Burke or Roger Scruton, who were capable of historicization. But in the hands of a conservative traditionalist, historicization is often used to insulate hierarchical forms of traditionalism from dispute, arguing they embody a kind of embedded wisdom and accomplishment that should only be challenged in exceptional moments. But for Brooks, the recognition that many traditions contain deep wisdom was never accompanied by the dogmatic compulsion to revere them as settled and beyond contestation. After all, one man's venerable tradition was another's dominating hegemony. In this respect conservative historicization has a distinctly politically correct quality to it, in always attempting to justify the present to men rather than calling on us – to invoke Marx in the *Theses on Feuerbach* – to change it.

Michael Brooks' Cosmopolitan Socialism II

To truly historicize a political question was to reveal not just the wisdom and insight brought to the table by different participants, but also their all too human failings and even outright malice. In this respect he very much resembles St Augustine from our first chapter, whose belief that history constituted the unfurling will of God never led him to revere the rust of antiquity or an unjust kingdom as anything more than a band of robbers. The same attitude stamps the work of Michael's hero, Cornel West. Seen from this perspective historization not only highlights the particularity of any political question and the actors therein, but retains that particularity within the more universal humanist narrative of our shared struggle for justice and a life of flourishing. Michael's cosmopolitan disposition recognized the humanity and dignity of Brazilian workers organizing behind Lula to combat some of the starkest inequality in developing Latin America, along with the demands of Bernie Sanders' campaign to provide decent living conditions for the poor in the richest country on Earth. He was as baffled by a militant Israeli ultra-nationalism, backed by American power, which failed to recognize the shared humanity of the Palestinian people under the occupation of the IDF as he was by the competitive market fundamentalism and "Me First" attitude of neoliberal globalization. Michael recognized the complex histories which gave birth to these global issues and movements, while still always taking the side of the least well off in every moment.

This disposition contributed to a healthy inclination to avoid giving in to some of the more hermetic and unhelpful forms of leftism out there today. Michael Brooks had little interest in the parochial argument that the struggles of one people were none of his business, or that one should refrain from examining and learning from them in a respectful manner. Indeed his knowledge of history's fluidity meant he always insisted that the very idea that we were simply one people or another was highly artificial. Where would the "Western" world be without the accomplishment of Arabic mathematicians? Why should generations of undergraduates have to find clever ways to pretend they read Aristotle rather than clever ways to pretend to read Confucius? This is what made him a model cosmopolitan socialist. As Michael put it near the conclusion of *Against the Web:*

...Much of the "ancient western tradition" was in fact highly geographically and intellectually diverse and included African and pan-Asian sources that are misleadingly remembered – and misleadingly whitened – as merely "Greek" or "Roman." But to underline the larger point I am trying to make: Instead of policing each other's influences and enjoyments for evidence of "cultural appropriation," we should all strive to emulate the curiosity and rigor of the great Christian revolutionary intellectual Cornel West, who explores the echoes between Anton Chekhov and the blues with no interest in drawing artificial lines between cultures.

Unfortunately, Michael's all too early death means he never got the opportunity – one he richly deserved – to spell out a lengthy principled justification for cosmopolitan socialism. Shortly before the end he laid out four central pillars he believed would be crucial:

1. Anti-Essentialism: essentialism asserts that there are characteristics of all members in a group share, by which they are defined (exemplified by the peerless work of Adolph Reed Jr and other for-real Marxist thinkers).
2. Internationalism – not only are we all in this together, the rest of the world has much to teach the United States; let's do a reverse shift in power and deeply learn from and cohere with the rest of the world.

3. Building a healthy culture, the left has many toxicities that can and often do make it a terrible place to be and not connected to the rest of the world; there is a class critique of this, which scholars like Vivek Chibber describes, and there is a spiritual psychological dimension. The left needs to learn from and engage in these traditions and in movements like liberation theology, we need to be able to deal with real human complicity and be good to each other.
4. Getting real about ideology and where it comes from so we can do a serious and grounded analysis of the world. Historical and material.

I've already discussed the point about anti-essentialism earlier in this chapter, and much of the prior two were taken up by analyzing the material and ideological dimensions of the world and the barriers to achieving cosmopolitan socialism. Below, I will discuss the principles and strategies that should define socialist internationalism, before concluding with what a healthy and spiritually rich left might look like.

Brooks' humanist disposition for cosmopolitan socialism recalls Terry Eagleton's well-known maxim in *Ideology* that a "socialist is just someone who is unable to get over his or her astonishment that most people who have lived and died have spent lives of wretched, fruitless, unremitting toil." This point is also echoed by another of Brook's heroes, Amartya Sen, whose capabilities approach to human freedom provides a loose index on what people genuinely need to lead flourishing lives. This is indeed a good starting point; far too many progressive intellectuals give remarkably technical justifications for their political standpoints while never acknowledging that the urge to humanize the world is first and foremost an affective one. Indeed if we take the Humean point about the centrality of the passions seriously, all our moral inclinations have their start in such passions. But we need to go further than that and provide a more rigorous theoretical justification for the cosmopolitan disposition which can withstand the inevitable objections which will be leveled against it. And from these theoretical justifications we can begin to speculate more concretely on what kind of institutions and practices will be necessary to bring about a proximate cosmopolitan socialist order. In a Marxist vein we should also recognize that any such effort will have to simultaneously build on what came before, while radicalizing its immanent tendencies for democratic and egalitarian purposes.

Arguing for Cosmopolitan Socialism from a Marxist Standpoint

Any theoretical justification for cosmopolitan socialism will undoubtedly end up owing a huge debt to Marxism; both the work of Marx himself and the many innovations developed by Marxists in the 2 centuries since he wrote. Marx's work reached the nadir of its influence at the end of the Cold War, when the faux triumphalism of neoliberalism and neoconservatism assumed the specter of his critique had been banished forever. Had these critics looked more carefully at his work, they ironically might have been immunized against this temptation. They'd have recognized that the creative destructive character of global capitalism inexorably revolutionized society, and consequently brought about the emergence of new contradictions and attendant social tensions. And they would have recognized that the pacification of workers' movements and radicals was bought at the price of sublimating capitalism ideologically and withdrawing it from political contestation through law. This simultaneously disconnected the economic defenders of capitalism from an awareness of its ground level impact through a withdrawal into abstract monetarism and a fixation on fictitious capital, limiting their ability to either predict mounting crises or recognize the political dimensions of economic affairs. They also failed to see how the effort to insulate the market from democratic deliberation would eventually produce anger and backlash, particularly once the promises of endless economic growth and rising living conditions turned out to mean high levels of job precarity and stagnating or falling real wages and inequality spiked drastically. Consequently the twenty-first century has seen Marx's reputation restored, though he remains ever controversial even among his disciples.

There are many different flavors of Marxism out there, some more compatible with humanistic cosmopolitan socialism than others. Fundamental to Marx's outlook was a commitment to a Hegelian notion of freedom as reciprocal self-determination. Put more simply, Marx rejected the idea that freedom simply meant each individual doing as they desired without inhibition within the boundaries of liberal law – the "negative liberty" so cherished by possessive individualist forms of liberalism. This is not because the liberties demanded by liberals were unimportant, which is a mistake some of the curter Marxists make. Even in "On the Jewish Question" – usually taken as his premiere statement of contempt for liberal rights – Marx emphasizes the importance of political toleration and even critiques Bruno Bauer for demanding Jews assimilate before being granted full citizenship rights. Throughout his work one can find expressions of support for freedom of expression and assembly, thoughts on how to advance pro-worker reforms through the institutions of representative democracy and the party system and more. But the negative liberties are insufficient because they retain a system of "possessive individualism" wherein some groups in society are able to live off of the alienated labor of others in the pursuit of profit. This flowed from early possessive individualist liberalism's extraordinarily expansive conception of private property, which only expanded further in the neoliberal era. A society, and indeed a global community, predicated on the few living off of the alienated labor of the many would always constrain our capacity to be freely self-determining.

This is firstly because it meant a majority of people would never have access to the kinds of material resources fully needed to live a life of flourishing, even though we could very easily provide them. The logic of the market precludes socializing resources in this way, and consequently allows them to inefficiently concentrate in the hands of a few. Secondly, Marx argues that the kinds of inequities in power and status generated by capitalist possessive individualism alienate us from one another and from our lifeworld. There are many different ways this kind of alienation occurs; the alienation of workers from each other through competition for jobs and status, alienation between workers and capitalists as a result of disparities in power, and of course the alienation of developed from developing countries. But at the root of all of them is a Hegelian sense that a lack of freedom for some means a lack of freedom for all. Or as Marx put it, "the free development of each is a condition for the free development of all." One way to understand this is systematically; to the extent we are all interpellated into naturalized capitalist dynamics which are framed as being beyond human control and even understanding, we will continue to feel alienated from the world and each other. Lastly, a third way in which capitalism constrains our ability to be self-determining is how it inhibits the process of mutual recognition necessary to develop a sufficiently strong sense of self-worth and identity to resist domination. Marx's crucial psychological insight is how we depend on other people to develop a sense of self-worth and identity over time, which goes well beyond the manic pursuit of commodified desire that defines capitalist morality. In the alienated and competitive world we live in, we are often unable to build that sense of self-worth and identity because we are denied the meaningful relationships with others which are its prerequisite. Instead we have the warre of all against all which has merely been moderated through the further coercion of the state. In this context we lack a sufficiently robust ego to resist conforming to ideology and the kinds of disciplinary interpellation that defined neoliberal post-modernity. The solution to this can only be a more democratic form of life where we construct a shared world together as equals.

Conceived in this way Marx's critique of capitalism still provides vital moral resources in framing the ways our freedom as self-determination is impaired under existent conditions. Beyond that there are many features of his description of capitalism's "laws of motion" which remain vital to our analysis of the present. His account of how capitalism constitutes a global system which transcends the boundaries of the nation-state is more relevant than ever before. Marx's theorizing on the "general intellect" and the transition from an industrial to a knowledge economy in *Grundrisse* has deservingly been credited with some major insights. *Capital: Volume Three*'s account of how fictitious capital is formed and becomes a dominant fetish remains a reservoir of insight that has not been fully tapped. And above all else Marx's arguments about ideology and the fetishized forms it assumes in the cultural lifeworld and even in our sense of identity have proven one of his most enduring legacies. It should come as no surprise that the most creative and active prongs of contemporary Marxist theorizing continue to build upon and deepen his analysis of ideology.

But there are elements of the Marxist tradition which should also be eschewed by cosmopolitan socialists. One of the most important is its unhelpful propensity toward class reductionism, which too many twenty-first century Marxists claim isn't a thing even as they ignore all other forms of power and domination that don't have to do with capitalist economics. In the past it was put forward that class was more foundational than all other intersectional forms of subjectivization because it was universal and so therefore had greater emancipatory potential; unlike race, for example. But as mentioned earlier, the rejection of these kinds of universalizing essentialisms is one of the key achievements of an otherwise flawed militant particularism. It is simply untrue that class is more universal or foundational than other kinds of identities interpellated by power. Consider how the feminist movement has come to challenge not just patriarchy, but all kinds of gendered identity power relations – including those impacting cis-gendered heterosexual men. Or how ubiquitous questions of cultural and religious identity have become, and their surprising resilience against vulgar materialist reductionism. The kind of universalism we require is a moral humanistic one; not one based on the idea that class activism alone can emancipate us all. Related to this would be weaning ourselves off of all kinds of economistic reductionism in our description of power; and yes that includes in the "last instance."

Secondly, the teleological interpretation many read into Marx's theory of history needs to be chucked like a bad habit. For some, this will be a very difficult pill to swallow. The more grandiose forms of Marxism out there tend to insist that if they cannot make predictions about capitalism's demise, then Marx is reduced down to little more than another moral critic of capitalism. This always has the further negative impact of gutting Marxists' capacity to say capitalism's downfall is imminent whether one likes it or not, so best to just get on board. To put it cheekily, without its teleological vision of history some will feel we remove what made Marxism special to the left. Ironically enough this often has more of a Messianic feel than anything else; a need to invest one's self in a triumphalist prophecy which predicts the inexorable overcoming of oppression and the rise of the city of brotherly love on Earth. In these extreme instances one is tempted to point such Marxists to all the Christian groups down the millennia who have claimed the end is nigh as a warning.

More sophisticated critics in the same vein might follow Althusser in arguing that a humanist Marxism stripped of the full scale "science of history" and its predictive power is no Marxism at all. It is at best a kind of left or young Hegelianism with a few proto-materialist insights. But I don't think this objection is ultimately sound. After 2 centuries it has become clear that capitalism has demonstrated an extraordinary adaptability; a capacity to reinvent itself that would make David Bowie proud. In some ways acknowledging this is more in line with the analytical stringency of Marx's analysis of capitalist political economy than foregrounding his rather speculative predictions about its oncoming demise. As an overdetermined social system with many contradictory dynamics, global capitalism isn't subject to the kind of large-scale predictive analysis teleological Marxists want to subject it to. Marx's critique of political economy is powerful because it allows us to dialectically understand the development and operation of capitalism in the past and present. Not because it makes anyone a seer. At best we may be able to make local and short-term speculations about the way one or another of capitalism's tendencies and contradictions will be materially instantiated. If that is unpalatable, there are always careers in fortune telling available. There is also a longstanding problem with treating Marxism solely as analytic for making historical predictions, which is that it can gut our capacity to engage in self-determining historical actions. If it is true that everything unfolds according to the deterministic logic of a materialist dialectic, it becomes unclear what role actual human beings and their choices are to play.

Finally, we need to rid ourselves of the longstanding temptation to view Marxism as a militantly anti-liberal, anti-humanist and purely revolutionary movement. This was a position often taken by Marxist-Leninists through the twentieth century. With the more "scientific" Marxists, they rejected the soft and reformist quality of any kind of socialist humanism as too moralistic and beholden to the limitations of bourgeois ideology. But they also eschewed the claim that one needs to dogmatically follow the deterministic logic of "science" without taking historical agency into one's own hands. The solution often given was that where an overdetermined system looks unlikely to crumble of its own accord anytime soon, it simply needs a "push." This has obviously been attractive to the most militant of activists in seeming to eschew both reformism and scientific withdrawal into mere theorizing. But it has also led to the most anti-dialectical approaches to the development of socialist relations. Its conception of radicality is not to transform the world from the base upwards, let alone to build democratic legitimacy for a transition toward more egalitarian material relations. Instead it licenses a vanguard movement to uproot everything in a process of creative destruction and apparently liberating violence. Partially as a result of its influence, we've seen the emergence of some of the most brutal totalitarian regimes the world has ever seen, and it is long past time the left stopped apologizing and whitewashing them.

What a cosmopolitan socialism should do is argue for the ongoing moral relevance of Marx's vision of human emancipation from capitalist alienation while carrying forward the most enduring virtues of his critique of political economy. Ultimately the most useful tool Marx provides is the contingency exposed by his historicizing critique of political economy, revealing economic relations to be historical rather than natural and very much responsible for creating an ideological horizon which calcifies our vision of possible futures. It does not offer a blueprint for how to get there, let alone suggest the wheels of history will simply bring us victory whether we will it into being or not.

Arguing for Cosmopolitan Socialism from a Moral Standpoint

One of the most frustrating features of Marx's legacy has been the propensity to see moral argumentation as little more than a kind of moralism. This has its roots in Marx and Engels' absolutely scathing denunciation of the utopian socialists, who drew up many idiosyncratic blueprints in the name of competing visions of justice. Marx and Engels were undoubtedly right to observe that any effort to simply reconceive the world without first understanding it was doomed to not change anything at all. Writing "recipes for the cook shops" of the future wasn't their ambition. But one of the consequences of their anti-moralism was the presumption that turning to any kind of substantial moral argumentation constituted a kind of descent into ahistorical abstraction. Or worse still, it broke the link between theory and praxis which made Marxism distinctive and was the source of much of its power. If the immanent laws of motion of capitalism are going to bring about socialism and then communism one way or another, there is little point in arguing about its morality. History itself becomes the great legitimator. Ironically, despite their often trenchant critiques of precisely these deterministic ambitions, most forms of left-wing critical theory and post-structuralism perpetuated this disinterest to moral argumentation. Scour the work of Deleuze, Foucault or Lyotard and you will find very few references to the ideal of justice. Adorno, Derrida and Spivak occasionally flirted with the language of morality, but always taking care to avoid substantiating the ideal of justice by giving it theoretical determinacy and precision. The result has been an impoverishment of left-wing critical theory, which often mechanically turns to the apparently self-evidently worthy principles of "emancipation," "radical democratization" or respect for difference as a justification for its policies. We must do better.

One place to start would be observing that any cosmopolitan socialism cannot be parochial in its moral concerns. Any cosmopolitanism worthy of the name will have to morally prioritize individuals beyond just the boundaries of one's nation-state, though in what way and to what extent will inevitably be controversial questions. My argument will be that we start from the egalitarian standpoint of arguing that each individual possesses equal moral worth to everyone else. This modernist principle has deep roots in the cosmopolitan Stoic tradition, the Buddhist egalitarian ethic, many branches of Christianity, and of course the best versions of liberalism and socialism. The argument for equal moral worth is essential for breaking us out of the idea that our exclusive duties are to ourselves, or that there is a class of more worthy individuals who are consequently worthy of much more than others.

The argument for the equal moral worth has two prongs, both of which have a broadly left-Kantian flavor. Firstly, we deny that there are any intrinsic qualities which make any individual *a priori* more morally worthy than any other. This was of course eminently contested by inegalitarians through the centuries; from Plato's insistence that some souls are more beautiful than others, through the belief that God or the gods organize people hierarchically according to what we deserve, down through the far more insidious kinds of essentialism about racial, gender and sexual inferiority. But neither these religious nor naturalizing arguments for inequality are particularly convincing anymore. Both depend on reading into individuals essentialized qualities which are intrinsically more worthy or less worthy than those belonging to others. Any reasonably modern materialism would argue that this ascribes metaphysical properties to matter which it does not have outside the judgments of human actors. Much like a fork is no less worthy than a spoon, and indeed neither are a fork nor a spoon outside the functional and linguistics meanings we ascribe to pieces of forged metal, there is nothing material that simply makes someone better than anyone else as a brute fact.

The idea that there is nothing which makes an individual *a priori* more morally worthy than another isn't to deny that there are other kinds of inequalities between people. Indeed recognizing this is foundational to both material analysis and the argument for socialism. One of the most obvious in an inequality in human capabilities. That some people are less capable of leading a life of human flourishing than others, whether because they were born into a family lacking social standing and resources due to a long history of poverty, or they came into the world with a serious and genetic medical problem, or they're a member of a long marginalized group, is a brutal fact of our existence. The argument that some people are more capable than others is usually appealed as a justification for neoliberal and other forms of meritocracy, which hold that people may not be intrinsically unequal, but will become so through competition with others where their merits and demerits will conform to patterns of rising and falling. The analogy given is typically to a race. But the reality is this meritocratic mythology is not much more convincing than the argument for intrinsic differences in moral worth. This is because the different capabilities that we have at best flow from morally arbitrary circumstances, and at worst are the result of long histories of injustice. Someone born with a genetic defect which leaves them unable to walk or work easily is no more responsible for their situation than a man born with remarkable physical and mental abilities. Both are the result of a mere genetic lottery. It is also a lottery that decides whether we are born into affluent or impoverished social circumstances, which play a huge role in determining where we end up. But even more than the biological issue, this lottery is much loaded and skewed by long histories of patriarchal, racial, classist and sexual oppression. To even talk about rising or falling based on something as mysterious as "merit" in such circumstances is beyond odd. So one of the arguments for a cosmopolitan socialism would of course be that, since there are no intrinsic differences in moral worth between people and the differences between human capabilities are either arbitrary or the result of often brutal histories of marginalization, it is wrong for some people to have fewer opportunities to live a life of flourishing than others.

One final and more complex issue pertains to inequalities of moral worth that are neither intrinsic nor related to capabilities, but concern personal virtue and moral excellence. Yes, we might say that there is nothing that naturally makes anyone more valuable than anyone else and yes it seems obvious that a lot or almost all of the differences in capability result from arbitrariness or marginalization. But what about the differences between a good and a bad person? Aren't those morally relevant when assessing the worth of an individual? This is a difficult question since much turns on one's definition of personal virtue, which cultural distinctions also play a part in. For Aristotle, the good and virtuous man looked a great deal like an Athenian aristocrat. To Benjamin Franklin, he was a thrifty and industrious WASP. Some contemporary defenders of virtue, like Alasdair Macintyre in his book *After Virtue*, acknowledge this difficulty and argue that there is no external set of criteria through which we can assess what constitutes a universal set of virtues. Everything is internal to the kinds of practices we engage in, which are further embedded in specific intellectual and cultural traditions. There is something to this, but I think this goes too far in the direction of cultural relativism. While we may not be able to establish an uncontroversial list of virtues, it seems clear that there are some kinds of personal virtue or rot that are universally admirable or damning. It would be a committed relativist indeed who would argue that whether Martin Luther King or Heinrich Himmler led a virtuous life depended exclusively on the internal criteria of the practice, as further set by one's cultural tradition. It may simply be that when it comes to universally establishing what counts as personal virtue, we must begin by negatively establishing what criteria – like Nazi criteria – cannot count.

The argument that some people are more morally virtuous and consequently lead more excellent lives does seem compelling. But I don't think a great deal turns on it from a socialist egalitarian standpoint. The argument that we should all possess whatever resources are needed to lead a flourishing life complements the claim that pursuing moral excellence and virtue is good, since as has been known since Aristotle, a person who lacks these resources will be seriously impeded in the striving to be good. Material necessity imposes stark pressures on all of us which compel moral compromises in order to survive, which in a neoliberal age increasingly includes even the most well off who nonetheless still need to compete with one another at a very high level. Indeed one argument against neoliberalism is that its anti-social hyper-competitiveness precludes the formation of virtue and the pursuit of excellence, since neither has much to do with developing our human capital.

The second argument for equal moral worth is that each person's life is as valuable to them as anyone else's life is to themselves. What I mean by this is as follows. Simple matter, including the matter of our bodies and brains, has no intrinsic worth in and of itself. Matter comes to matter because it is ascribed worth by self-conscious subjects for a nearly infinite variety of reasons. The first thing we come to value is of course our own conscious existence within the world, which is a precondition for our coming to ascribe worth to anything else. One dimension of being not just conscious but self-conscious is precisely this reflective transition to seeing myself not just as an experiencing ego, but an "I" for whom I am responsible. To put it in the more phenomenological language of Heidegger in *Being and Time*, our existential primordiality is care and the first thing we care about is our selves. This is not to suggest that all we are is this self-conscious "I," however, which would very quickly lead to a kind of transcendental solipsism. One of the virtues of the phenomenological tradition, particularly Heidegger and Merleau Ponty, is to stress how the "I" comes to take an intentionalist stance toward the world seemingly outside of itself, primarily mediating between the two through the body. My care for myself comes to extend to the care I have for the various projects engaged in within the world, whether for mere survival or more elaborate enterprises. Over time this imbues the world with meaning and significance where it has none as mere matter.

As Marx and others would remind us, though, one of the most significant moments in this process is the recognition of other self-conscious beings in the world. This raises profound existential questions about the status of other minds, whether our different projects can be compatible, and of course whether the respective meanings we ascribe to matter are the same. Much conflict results from this, not least when we enter into economic relations with one another that deny the self-conscious reality of other human beings by ascribing value only to their labor power and consequently reducing them into a fount for alienated production. To be treated in this manner – which goes under many different labels (being objectified, being dehumanized, being instrumentalized as a mere means to another's ends) – is one of the most haunting and damaging experiences a person can undergo. It is made all the more painful since it is not a purely natural phenomena but arises from the self-conscious decision of another who has chosen not to acknowledge our own self-conscious. In other words, to see their own life and projects as fundamentally or even absolutely more valuable than our own. Where Marx and Hegel fundamentally complete the more subjectivist tale given by Kant, Ponty and others is forcing us to recognize the self-consciousness of other humans as being of equal moral significance to our own. Or to invert Gabriel Guy Marquez, it is not enough that I exist and flourish at this moment if you do not as well.

Of course this is by no means easy, and much of human political and personal life is taken up with the task. What makes post-modern phenomena like New Age spiritualism cringey is precisely how it suggests there are easy or commodified fixes to the problem. While they often lacked a firm conception of moral rightness to guide us, what critical theorists at their best provided were elaborate accounts for how many psychic and ideological barriers exist to recognizing the self-consciousness of others as being of equal moral significance as our own. And again, what makes neoliberalization conservatism noxious is how they direct us toward a manically solipsistic vision of the world where the only thing that matters is developing my personal human capital so as to pursue my own projects my own way, which will include the instrumentalization of others on as broad a scale as possible. What gives this a perverse quality is, in a world where we are so often denied recognition from others and do not give it ourselves, the result is a loss of meaning. Anxious and dependent only on ourselves, our whole sense of the world's significance comes to turn on how much power we can acquire to will our own projects into being. But since these projects matter only to ourselves, and no one else, even accomplishing them is a kind of impotent grandeur; a Tower of Babel where the breakdown of intersubjective recognition and authentic speech means no one else can offer sincere praise, admiration or love. We can only look for affirmation from those whose equal humanity we have instrumentalized away, and consequently whose recognition comes to mean little or nothing to us. Under the conditions of neoliberal post-modernity we have accomplishment without significance, gain without wealth, and power without dignity. Post-modern conservatism arises as a reaction to these problems but offers only more radically inegalitarian and nihilistic paths forward.

What cosmopolitan socialism needs to achieve, therefore, is to create global material conditions where it becomes far easier to recognize the equal moral worth of all other individuals and enable us all to live mutually flourishing lives. How to do this is what I'll discuss next.

Building and Democratizing International Institutions

Concluding that each human life is of equal moral worth is foundational to the cosmopolitan socialist project. But it says little about what respecting the equal moral worth of all human beings practically entails. Fortunately, one of the immediate implications is that we should indeed be cosmopolitans. Beyond all the valid Marxist and critical analyses of the state and its violence one could make, we can insist there are no legitimate reasons for parochially narrowing our sense of moral obligation merely to those who happen to belong to the same nation-state as ourselves. Ascribing these arbitrary factors significant weight is parochial in that it circumscribes the range of our moral imaginations to those most proximate to ourselves geographically and politically. While there may be good circumstantial reasons for doing so in certain instances, these should not be elevated to the level of a stringent principle. Each human life has equal worth means all human lives have equal worth, including those which we may never see or whose lives it may be difficult to imagine.

The project of Kantian cosmopolitanism discussed in the first chapter held to this same ideal, even if it did not go far enough to materially instantiate it. It was formulated on the idea that the government of each state had a duty to all of its citizens to maintain the rightful condition for their flourishing, and where it failed to do so it lost legitimate sovereignty and became an outlaw regime. This is what occurred with the Nazis, Milosevic and the Khmer Rouge. Had we lived in a better world, it would have also been the fate of the Bush administration. The United Nations and the post-1949 regime of international human rights, the International Criminal Court and International Court of Justice, and the vast array of affiliated regulatory administrations and watchdogs, NGOS and activists are imperfect instruments in this regard. But they have nevertheless accomplished inspirational feats and retain the most legitimacy in the eyes of the world. One of the ambitions of cosmopolitan socialists should be to either govern or steer them in a more radical direction. Both by further constraining the hegemony and violence of states large and small, and through deconstructing the neoliberal regime of international law insulating capital from democratic pressures. This latter move should be accompanied by concurrent efforts to replace neoliberal international law with a legal order consistent with cosmopolitan socialist principles. In this respect we should take a page from the neoliberal playbook by recognizing that those kind of socialist reforms will not be safe in a purely domestic context but need to be complemented with international laws that insulate such regimes from capitalist pressure and provide them with legitimacy and aid. This would have to go well beyond efforts to codify economic and social rights circa the 1976 *International Covenant on Economic, Social, and Cultural Rights*, though its failures might provide some useful guidance.

There are some leftists who might object to these efforts along several different lines. The most acute post-colonial and TWAIL critics of international law, like Muthucumaraswamy Sornarajah or Anthony Anghie, will likely and understandably remain deeply suspicious that international law can be reformed and radicalized this way. They will see it as too fundamentally embedded in a history of colonial practices and discourses, and consequently inextricable from contemporary systems of domination. I will try to answer this objection below where I argue for establishing more deliberative and robust chains of democratic deliberation to legitimate international law and institutions and ensure it is more responsive to the demos and less to global elites. But another objection might come from more traditional socialists like John Judis, author of *The Socialist Awakening*. Judis argues that young socialists have made a big mistake in embracing "anti-patriotic" internationalism. They embrace policies about open borders for high levels of immigration, obligations abroad, and are wary of economic nationalism. This means they miss a crucial opportunity to convert their fellow citizens, who may be open to the idea of egalitarian economic reform but want the beneficiaries to be people like them. Judis argues that politicians like Jeremy Corbyn and Bernie Sanders were initially successful in part because they appealed to this patriotic urge, and only stumbled when treading into the unhelpful waters of internationalism.

I think this is very mistaken on several levels. Beyond just our moral obligation to respect the equal worth of all individuals, which should be enough in and of itself, there are good tactical reasons to be wary of Judis's position. Firstly, the kind of nation-state driven socialism Judis argues for was tried many times through the twentieth century, and it inevitably ran into both severe economic limitations and intense pressure for militant capitalist states. There is no reason to suppose the same would not happen again. Secondly, the reason why the more admirable institutions and policies advanced by socialists before the 1980s fell apart was because of a coordinated and global assault by neoliberals, who were able to reform international laws and outlooks to put intense competitive pressure on welfarism and domestic workers movements. The same problems will emerge with a twenty-first century nation-state driven socialism. And thirdly, the flip side of this coin is that constructing solidarity across borders and building a global coalition to deconstruct neoliberal internationalism and replace it with something better is far more likely to secure broad legitimation for its aims and permanent accomplishments in the long run. Even far-right nationalist movements have recognized that there is no retreating from the world anymore and have set up a vast array of think tanks, activist movements and digital rallying sites to promote their cause. The left must do the same and do far better.

The key way to secure legitimation for such a global project is indeed through solidaristic internationalism, though it must be channeled in the direction of permanent institutional construction and reform. One of the problems with leftist movements through the 2010s was that they were often able to electrify global conscience, if one thinks of Occupy Wall Street or Black Lives Matter, but rarely left lasting institutions behind. We need to do far better. Chains of democratic legitimation need to be established, whereby the interests and goals of activists are channeled into local and domestic civil society organizations which permanently advocate on behalf of the base while encouraging deliberation and participation in the formulation of principles and prescriptions.

These should link up with sister organizations in other countries, to work in tandem to push the most well-established liberal and left-liberal international institutions in more radical directions. While there is some of this going on over issues like the Israeli-Palestinian conflict and climate change, it needs to become more permanent and formalized while always remaining responsive and flexible given the needs on the ground. At the same time democratic socialist movements should aim to win and hold state power, and then use that to further empower domestic civil society organizations sympathetic to our cause while championing their ambition to pressure international institutions. Eventually the goal should be to capture and govern those institutions and use them to build a more inclusive international legal architecture that foregrounds putting constraints on the power of imperialist states and capital, incorporates the voices of the global south in a far more substantive way, and promotes far more robust forms of development aid and redistribution from the rich to the poor both within and between states.

This approach should be acceptable to post-colonial critics but will naturally be resisted very staunchly by the political right; both in its pro-capitalist and nationalist wings. This raises a substantial problem since any democratic socialism will have to allow these groups to continue playing a role in domestic and international politics. It becomes doubly problematic since the right has, ironically, tended to be better at thinking globally than the militant-particularist left. This means powerful conservative states will resist efforts to build the kind of movements described every step of the way; including through violence, as the long history of American imperialism in Latin America testifies to. One way to inhibit this will be to impose regulatory restrictions on the sources of funding and influence that fuel the political right and doing so in the name of democracy. Limiting the influence of money in democratic politics through imposing restrictions on campaign donations and corruption, breaking up the influence of monopolistic firms, and establishing a more robust set of think tanks, advocacy groups and influencers to compete with conservatives will all be vital. But most important of all will simply be presenting a more inspiring future than that offered by the right. This is where we turn to how cosmopolitan socialists should think of material equality.

Securing Global Equality

Michael Brooks and I shared an interest in the work of Amartya Sen, an Indian economist whose early work focused on famines but who later transitioned to writing about what he called the "capabilities approach" to human freedom and flourishing. This was later expertly elaborated on by the liberal feminist theorist and classicist Martha Nussbaum. The basic idea of the capabilities approach is to provide a more materialist account of what is required to lead an emancipated and rich human life than what one finds in the classical liberal tradition, with its fetishization of mere negative liberty. Each individual may possess more or less capabilities to pursue their vision of the good life – what Mill would call experiments in living – than the others, with constraints and limitations being imposed by material conditions and domination by all forms of power. Someone committed to the moral equality of human beings would of course want each individual to be as capable of experimenting with their life to achieve the good as possible, and so seek to maximize everyone's capabilities to the extent possible. They would also look very critically at any system which enabled wealth and resources to accumulate at the top, enabling both the formation of systems of domineering power and failing to grant individuals what they need to flourish when the resources are available. There is also a deep affinity, though too rarely stated by Sen and Nussbaum, between their position and the humanistic emphasis on developing human powers to flourish in Marx.

While Sen and Nussbaum have always been too blasé about the power dynamics of political economy, often accepting a relatively uncontroversial left-liberal take inspired by Adam Smith, their theorizing on capabilities provides the left with an extremely helpful index on what all human beings need to live a flourishing life. Sen has always been reluctant to state what the most important capabilities should be, since doing so might decontextualize our interpretation. But fortunately, in her book *Creating Capabilities*, Martha Nussbaum has been more willing to provide some clarity. Her index of capabilities is ranked by priority, and includes:

1. Life: Being able to live to the end of a human life of normal length.

2. Bodily Health: Being able to have good health.

3. Bodily Integrity: Being able to move freely from place to place, security and opportunities for sexual satisfaction and reproduction.

4. Senses, Imagination and Thought: Being able to use one's senses, imagine, think and reason and to have these cultivated by an education and participatory culture. Being able to have pleasurable experiences.

5. Emotions: Being able to have attachments to things and people outside of ourselves and to not have one's emotional development blighted by fear and anxiety.

6. Practical reason: Being able to form a conception of the good and engage in reflection on it.

7. Affiliation: A) Being able to live with and toward others, to have institutions that foster this and B) Having the social bases for people to possess self-respect and not be subjected to humiliation.

8. Other Species: Being able to live with concern for and in relation to animals, plants and the world of nature.

9. Play: Being able to laugh, play and enjoy recreation.

10. Control Over One's Environment: A) Political-Being able to participate in political choices that govern one's life, participate in politics, free speech. B) Material-Being able to hold property and enjoy property rights on an equal basis with each other, to be protected against search and seizure, to engage in work and enjoy meaningful relationships with other workers.

This index is indeed rich and suggestive and provides a guide to what cosmopolitan socialists should be trying to achieve for all through the institutional and political changes discussed last section. But we do need to offer some criticisms. Firstly, and related to the limits of their critique of political economy, Sen and Nussbaum take an unduly narrow and classical liberal approach to conceiving political participation. It is no coincidence that "control over one's environment" has the lowest priority on Nussbaum's index. This is extremely problematic since she fails to appreciate how a failure to prioritize political participation from the demos contributes to maintaining inegalitarian material systems and power relations. The ability to "participate in political choices that govern one's life" is not simply a luxury that comes after securing the other capabilities. It is a necessary perquisite for both demanding a rich set of capabilities for all and ensuring that the institutions constructed to provide them are maintained and secure against interferences. This is where the importance of democracy and democratization is so important as a means of pushing against neoliberal depoliticization and the insulation of capital from the demos. Here we also have to push very hard on what constitutes the proper domain of politics. As a feminist Nussbaum rightly emphasizes that being able to participate in choices within the family are a necessary human capability. But she says very little about the prospect of workplace democracy and the transition from ownership by capitalists to governance by workers. We should be very critical on this point and argue that in addition to needing to place far more priority on democratic political participation, this must be extended to allowing workers a far greater and ultimately primary say in how the corporations they are members of are organized and directed. This would have the added effect of ensuring greater returns to the economically marginalized than to capital.

Secondly, we need to radicalize Nussbaum's Rawlsian arguments about the "social bases" of self-respect. From a classical liberal standpoint, these social bases amount to enjoying freedom under the law and within the market. Sen and Nussbaum rightly draw our attention to the fact that far more is needed, since someone living in material deprivation naturally lacks a basis for self-respect relative to their peers. But flowing from the democratic point, we need to recognize that included in the social bases of self-respect should be an understanding that each of us is as capable of having a say in the political institutions which govern us as anyone else. This doesn't mean that everyone will or must exercise these capabilities, but they should be available. One of the tremendous catalysts for post-modern conservative nationalism has been the sense that the nation-state is no longer responsive to the needs of "ordinary citizens." This has often been cast in a racist and bigoted way. But the solution isn't to withdraw from democratization, but from populism. Populism holds that the "real people" as determined by a leader who speaks for them should be in charge. Democracy holds that all who are reasonably impacted by a political order should directly participate in its operations and determine the laws which flow from them. In this way we become not just atomized individuals pursuing our separate ambitions, but citizens constructing a shared world together. This provides a far firmer social basis for self-respect than mere formal equality under the benevolent auspices of liberal law and its possessive individualism.

Accompanied by these theoretical reorientations the goal of a cosmopolitan socialism should be to organize international institutions to secure a relatively equal index of human capabilities – or something rather like the index – for all. What this entails will naturally depend a great deal on both individual needs and social circumstances. One of the virtues of the capabilities approach is its conceptual and moral flexibility on these points, which makes it perfectly suited to a cosmopolitan project. For example, in the United States the most pressing matter when securing bodily health for all will naturally be establishing a universal public health care system. That wouldn't be as pressing an issue in a country with public health systems like Cuba, where securing more robust democratic and political rights would be more important. For sweat shop workers in Indonesia and Vietnam, securing capabilities of "play" through shortening the working day and week will undoubtedly be a priority. In many parts of sub-Saharan Africa securing both women's bodily health and capabilities to exercise practical reason will be dependent on ensuring everyone has access to safe, clean drinking water. This is because patriarchal gender norms create the expectation that it will primarily be girls who collect water, which can sometimes take hours a day and inhibit their ability to access education. The task of achieving equal capabilities of flourishing for all human beings is immeasurably complex, and one of the ongoing challenges to cosmopolitan socialism will be providing international steering in the right direction while maintaining sufficient ideological and institutional flexibility to enact the necessary reforms at the bottom.

The political right will no doubt dismiss this cosmopolitan vision as extravagantly utopian, while casually ignoring that it is their own efforts which go a long way to preventing its realization. Certainly the world that would emerge would be more just than the one we currently live in. But it would not be a utopia in the sense of a perfect world where everyone was happy and all experiments in living wound up successfully. It would still be one in which the tragedy of the human condition – its follies, petty vanities, personal failures, the transformation of love into hatred – were present. Many innocent people would still suffer, and death – necessary end though it may be – will still come for us all. Yet a cosmopolitan socialism would do much to rectify the needless suffering of the world and empower all individuals to pursue the highest ends in life to the extent that they are able. And it would enable us to foster and develop a broader range of human potential than ever before, ensuring that we do not lose the talents of a Michelangelo or a Frida to sweatshops and slums or worse.

Conclusion: Constructing a Shared World Together

The left has empathy but doesn't provide spiritual nourishment.
Reclaiming time is a way of enacting a different reality.
Michael Brooks

One area where the left has always been weak has been catering to the spiritual side of human nature. We are unrivaled in our capacity to provide materialist, discursive, deconstructive, genealogical and a million other flavors of critical analysis. Yet when it comes to offering inspiring visions of the future, let alone the highest ends to which our life should be set, we have often fallen short of the mark. The passing of Michael Brooks, one of the most spiritually attuned progressives, is made all the more tragic since we are bereft of his insight on these points. Great lives are like mirrors, in that they reflect our own life back to us more sharply and vividly that we're normally able to perceive. If there is anything we should learn from Michael it is how integrally his bottomless empathy was connected to his cosmopolitan curiosity at all human things, and his wish to see them become more of what they are. To realize the potentialities within and not have them squashed by poverty, power and prejudice.

At the individual level this aspiration to become more of what we are through empowered experiments reflects the idea that there are many worthy ends to which a life may be set. Some may choose to find meaning in aesthetic excellence, others scientific revelations, and of course romantic and familial love and mutual recognition. The finitude of time available to us may superficially appear tragic, but in fact compels us to choose which of these priorities matter the most to us. At the same moment we can find resonance and mutual recognition through the democratic construction of a shared world together. This would be a world unlike any other in human history, since it would finally reflect the belief that each individual life has a sacred dignity regardless of where we begin or the mistakes and failures we all make. The construction of a shared world does not mean it will be a perfect world, since we are all of us imperfect, and out of "the crooked timber of our humanity" nothing entirely straight will ever be made. But an imperfect world made by all of us would perfectly reflect who we are and what we intend to become. Not the Kingdom of God on Earth, but an Earth with no kingdoms at war and no life better not lived. I can think of no higher cause than that.

CULTURE, SOCIETY & POLITICS

Contemporary culture has eliminated the concept and public
figure of the intellectual. A cretinous anti-intellectualism
presides, cheer-led by hacks in the pay of multinational
corporations who reassure their bored readers that there is no
need to rouse themselves from their stupor. Zer0 Books knows
that another kind of discourse - intellectual without being
academic, popular without being populist - is not only possible:
it is already flourishing. Zer0 is convinced that in the unthinking,
blandly consensual culture in which we live, critical and engaged
theoretical reflection is more important than ever before.

If you have enjoyed this book, why not tell other readers by
posting a review on your preferred book site.

You may also wish to
subscribe to our Zer0 Books YouTube Channel.

Bestsellers from Zer0 Books include:

Give Them An Argument
Logic for the Left
Ben Burgis
Many serious leftists have learned to distrust talk of logic. This is
a serious mistake.
Paperback: 978-1-78904-210-8 ebook: 978-1-78904-211-5

Poor but Sexy
Culture Clashes in Europe East and West
Agata Pyzik
How the East stayed East and the West stayed West.
Paperback: 978-1-78099-394-2 ebook: 978-1-78099-395-9

An Anthropology of Nothing in Particular
Martin Demant Frederiksen
A journey into the social lives of meaninglessness.
Paperback: 978-1-78535-699-5 ebook: 978-1-78535-700-8

In the Dust of This Planet
Horror of Philosophy vol. 1
Eugene Thacker
In the first of a series of three books on the Horror of Philosophy,
In the Dust of This Planet offers the genre of horror as a way of
thinking about the unthinkable.
Paperback: 978-1-84694-676-9 ebook: 978-1-78099-010-1

The End of Oulipo?
An Attempt to Exhaust a Movement
Lauren Elkin, Veronica Esposito
Paperback: 978-1-78099-655-4 ebook: 978-1-78099-656-1

Capitalist Realism
Is There No Alternative?
Mark Fisher
An analysis of the ways in which capitalism has presented itself
as the only realistic political-economic system.
Paperback: 978-1-84694-317-1 ebook: 978-1-78099-734-6

Rebel Rebel
Chris O'Leary
David Bowie: every single song. Everything you want to know,
everything you didn't know.
Paperback: 978-1-78099-244-0 ebook: 978-1-78099-713-1

Kill All Normies
Angela Nagle
Online culture wars from 4chan and Tumblr to Trump.
Paperback: 978-1-78535-543-1 ebook: 978-1-78535-544-8

Cartographies of the Absolute
Alberto Toscano, Jeff Kinkle
An aesthetics of the economy for the twenty-first century.
Paperback: 978-1-78099-275-4 ebook: 978-1-78279-973-3

Malign Velocities
Accelerationism and Capitalism
Benjamin Noys
Long listed for the Bread and Roses Prize 2015, *Malign Velocities*
argues against the need for speed, tracking acceleration
as the symptom of the ongoing crises of capitalism.
Paperback: 978-1-78279-300-7 ebook: 978-1-78279-299-4

Meat Market
Female Flesh under Capitalism
Laurie Penny
A feminist dissection of women's bodies as the fleshy fulcrum of
capitalist cannibalism, whereby women are both consumers and
consumed.
Paperback: 978-1-84694-521-2 ebook: 978-1-84694-782-7

Babbling Corpse
Vaporwave and the Commodification of Ghosts
Grafton Tanner
Paperback: 978-1-78279-759-3 ebook: 978-1-78279-760-9

New Work New Culture
Work we want and a culture that strengthens us
Frithjof Bergmann
A serious alternative for mankind and the planet.
Paperback: 978-1-78904-064-7 ebook: 978-1-78904-065-4

Romeo and Juliet in Palestine
Teaching Under Occupation
Tom Sperlinger
Life in the West Bank, the nature of pedagogy and the role of a
university under occupation.
Paperback: 978-1-78279-637-4 ebook: 978-1-78279-636-7

Color, Facture, Art and Design
Iona Singh
This materialist definition of fine-art develops guidelines for
architecture, design, cultural-studies and ultimately social
change.
Paperback: 978-1-78099-629-5 ebook: 978-1-78099-630-1

Neglected or Misunderstood
The Radical Feminism of Shulamith Firestone
Victoria Margree
An interrogation of issues surrounding gender, biology,
sexuality, work and technology, and the ways in which our
imaginations continue to be in thrall to ideologies of maternity
and the nuclear family.
Paperback: 978-1-78535-539-4 ebook: 978-1-78535-540-0

How to Dismantle the NHS in 10 Easy Steps (Second Edition)
Youssef El-Gingihy
The story of how your NHS was sold off and why you will have
to buy private health insurance soon. A new expanded second
edition with chapters on junior doctors' strikes and government
blueprints for US-style healthcare.
Paperback: 978-1-78904-178-1 ebook: 978-1-78904-179-8

Digesting Recipes
The Art of Culinary Notation
Susannah Worth
A recipe is an instruction, the imperative tone of the expert, but
this constraint can offer its own kind of potential. A recipe need
not be a domestic trap but might instead offer escape – something
to fantasise about or aspire to.
Paperback: 978-1-78279-860-6 ebook: 978-1-78279-859-0

Most titles are published in paperback and as an ebook.
Paperbacks are available in traditional bookshops. Both print and
ebook formats are available online.
Follow us at:
https://www.facebook.com/ZeroBooks
https://twitter.com/Zer0Books
https://www.instagram.com/zero.books